PICTURING THE CENTURY

One Hundred Years of Photography from the National Archives

By

Bruce I. Bustard

National Archives and Records Administration
Washington, DC
in association with the University of Washington Press
Seattle and London

PUBLISHED BY THE NATIONAL ARCHIVES TRUST FUND BOARD
AND THE UNIVERSITY OF WASHINGTON PRESS

Copyright ©1999 by the University of Washington Press

Printed in Hong Kong

LIBRARY OF CONGRESS CATALOGING-IN-PUBLICATION DATA

Bustard, Bruce I., 1954–
    Picturing the century: one hundred years of photography from the National
Archives / Bruce I. Bustard.
      p.   cm.
    Catalog of an exhibition held at the National Archives and Records Administration in
Washington, DC from March 1999 to Jan. 2001.
    Includes bibliographical references and index.
    ISBN 0-295-97772-8 (alk. paper)
    1. United States. National Archives and Records Administration—Photograph collections—
Exhibitions. 2. Photograph collections—Washington (D.C.)—Exhibitions. 3. Photography—
United States—History—20th century—Exhibitions.   I. United States.   National Archives and
Records Administration.
    II. Title.
    TR6.U6W18   1999
    779'.997391'074753—dc21   98-44102
                                                    CIP

Designed by Janice Hargett, National Archives and Records Administration

The paper used in this publication meets the minimum requirements of the American National Standards for Permanence of Paper for Printed Library Materials Z39.48-1992.

Cover photo: See fig. 36
Back cover photos: See figs. 88, 26, 136, and 69

Contents

Preface   *v*

Acknowledgments   *vii*

Picturing the Century:
One Hundred Years of Photography from the National Archives   *1*

A New Century   *34*
   Portfolio: Walter Lubken   *46*
   Portfolio: Lewis Hine   *50*

The Great War & the New Era   *54*
   Portfolio: George Ackerman   *66*

The Great Depression & the New Deal   *70*
   Portfolio: Dorothea Lange   *80*
   Portfolio: Ansel Adams   *84*

A World in Flames   *88*
   Portfolio: Charles Fenno Jacobs   *98*

Postwar America   *102*
   Portfolio: Yoichi Okamoto   *112*

Century's End   *116*
   Portfolio: Danny Lyon   *132*

For Further Reading   *136*

THE 20TH CENTURY has seen striking technological progress, remarkable scientific and medical advances, the widespread growth of educational opportunities, and the spread of democracy. It has also seen sweeping social disruption, stifling ideological conformity, and death and destruction on horrific levels. One way to visualize and comprehend the variety of the last 100 years is through historic photographs. Photographers have recorded the century's major events and personalities on billions of images. This publication and the exhibit upon which it is based provide a selection of 20th century images from one of the largest photographic archives in the world—the National Archives and Records Administration (NARA).

Most people know NARA as the home of the Charters of Freedom: the Declaration of Independence, the Constitution of the United States, and the Bill of Rights. Visitors and researchers may also recall that the National Archives of the United States contains many other famous written records such as the Louisiana Purchase Treaty, the Emancipation Proclamation, and the World War II Japanese Instrument of Surrender. Beyond these landmark examples are billions of less well-known letters, public laws, memorandums, certificates, court decisions, military service records and passenger arrival lists.

Fewer people realize that NARA also has millions of photographs among its holdings. From its beginnings in the mid-1930s, the National Archives has also accessioned and preserved the permanently valuable visual record of Federal agencies. Over the years this responsibility has brought an ever-growing number of photographic prints, negatives, slides, and transparencies into NARA facilities in the Washington, DC, area as well as into NARA regional records facilities and Presidential libraries across the country.

To mark the end of the 20th century, we have brought together 157 of NARA's most interesting photographs in this publication. It is based on the NARA exhibit "Picturing the Century: One Hundred Years of Photography from the National Archives." The publication and exhibit explore the role of Government photography in the United States and illustrate the changes in American society over the last 100 years. They also showcase some of NARA's photographic riches and highlight the work of outstanding photographers such as Lewis Hine, Dorothea Lange, Ansel Adams, Edward Steichen, Russell Lee, Danny Lyon, and Yoichi Okamoto.

NARA's mission is to provide ready access to essential evidence that documents the rights of American citizens, the actions of Federal officials, and the national experience. The images in this publication are but a few of the national treasures held by NARA in its 33 facilities nationwide. I invite you to inspect for yourself the records of your Government by visiting our research facilities, participating in our educational programs, or viewing our exhibits. In our democracy the records that constitute the National Archives belong to all citizens. ■

JOHN W. CARLIN
Archivist of the United States

Acknowledgments

THIS CATALOG is based on the 1999 National Archives and Records Administration (NARA) exhibition "Picturing the Century: One Hundred Years of Photography from the National Archives." Both the catalog and the exhibition were prepared by staff members of NARA's Office of Records Services—Washington, DC under the direction of Michael J. Kurtz, Edith M. James, and Chris Rudy Smith. Michael L. Jackson designed the exhibit; James D. Zeender was the exhibit registrar; Thomas Nastick developed the exhibition video; Sarah Wagner was the chief exhibition conservator. Janice Hargett designed the exhibit catalog.

Outside of NARA, Bernard Mergan of The George Washington University; David E. Hamilton of the University of Kentucky; Lisa B. Auel of the Matheson Historical Center; Pete Daniel of the National Museum of American History; and the late Fredric M. Miller of the National Endowment for the Humanities gave of their time and expertise to review the exhibit script, the catalog, or both. Jamie Rosenfield assisted with the research for the exhibit and later organized the exhibit prints and negatives. Laurie Weiner of the White House Photo Office provided a selection of photographs from the Clinton Administration. Janel Showalter edited the manuscript with great care. The staff of the University of Washington Press, including Donald Ellegood, Pat Soubers, and Veronica Seyd, enthusiastically supported the catalog. As always, Tory Bustard patiently encouraged me while I completed this project.

At NARA in Washington, DC, Stacey Bredhoff, Cathy Farmer, Darlene McClurkin, Marilyn Paul, Ray Ruskin, Anne Eales, Benjamin Guterman, Maureen MacDonald, Robert Kvasnicka, Kenneth Heger, Nancy Malan, Robert E. Richardson, Alysha Black, Tracee Butler, Richard Hunt, Jeffrey Landou, Sandra Glasser, Sharon Thibodeau, Richard H. Smith, Laurie Baty, Susan Cooper, Bonnie Curtin, Edward McCarter, Kate Flaherty, Mary Ilario, Richard Boylan, Naomi Revzen, Jill Glenewinkel, Pat Eames, Douglas Thurman, Rutha Beamon, Sharon Culley, Holly Reed, and David Pfeiffer offered their assistance throughout the project. I am especially grateful to Richard Schneider, Steven Puglia, Mike Carter, Amy Young, and Cecilia Epstein who did most of the photography for the exhibit and the catalog and for the contribution of Nicholas J. Natanson. Nick critiqued the exhibit script and catalog drafts and answered my many questions about NARA's still photography holdings.

The audiovisual archivists at NARA's Presidential libraries were unfailingly helpful during the preparation of the exhibit and catalog, as well. My thanks go to Stephen Branch, Reagan Library; Mary Finch, Bush Library; Alan Goodrich, Kennedy Library; Kenneth Hafeli, Ford Library; Scott Nollen, Hoover Library; Mark Renovitch, Roosevelt Library; David Stanhope, Carter Library; Kathleen Struss, Eisenhower Library; Pauline Testerman, Truman Library; Philip Scott, Johnson Library; and Stephen H. Greene, Nixon Presidential Materials Project.

Archivists from NARA's regional records facilities also selected photographs from their holdings for consideration. Thanks go to Robert C. Morris, Northeast; Alan Perry, Central Plains; Mary Ann Hawkins, Southeast; Susan Karren, Pacific Alaska; Kent Carter and Meg Hacker, Southwest; James Mouat, Mid Atlantic; Peter Bunce, Great Lakes; Waverly Lowell, Pacific; and Joan Howard, Rocky Mountain.

As this list of names demonstrates, this project has been an enormously collaborative undertaking. I am grateful to all who assisted me with it. ∎

BRUCE I. BUSTARD, *Curator*

PICTURING THE CENTURY

One Hundred Years of Photography from the National Archives

IMMIGRANTS ARRIVING AT ELLIS ISLAND . . . THE WRIGHT BROTHERS' FIRST FLIGHT . . . BUILDING THE EMPIRE STATE BUILDING . . . A DEPRESSION-ERA SOUP LINE . . . OMAHA BEACH . . . THE MUSHROOM CLOUD . . . LYNDON JOHNSON TAKING THE PRESIDENTIAL OATH . . . A YOUNG MARINE IN DA NANG . . . FOOTPRINTS ON THE MOON . . . WAR IN THE PERSIAN GULF . . .

Old photographs are time machines. They allow us to look back in history, freeze a moment in time, and imagine ourselves as part of the past. Through photographs we can see how famous and ordinary folk appeared in both posed and unguarded moments. We can relive great events and everyday life in exquisite detail. We can tell how people dressed and carried themselves and sometimes judge their moods. Looking at historic photographs helps us imagine what it was like when the first airplane took off, when a landing craft ramp fell open on D-day, or when the first human being stepped onto the Moon.

But old photographs are also historical documents. They are more than just jumbles of detail—a new style of dress on the edge of an image, an old building on the right, a famous face in the center. They do more than illustrate, and they impart more than nostalgia. Photographs are created deliberately; they seek to convey meaning and suggest an interpretation of a particular moment in history. They are also the product of a complex interaction among the photographer, the subject, the viewer, and those who may have requested the image. In the words of photohistorian Alan Trachtenberg, photographs are "cultural texts" asking to be read and studied closely.

The events of the 20th century have been captured on billions of photographs. This explosion of images was largely made possible by technological advances in cameras, film, and film developing. During the 19th century, photography had been the exclusive province of professionals. Cameras were large and bulky; negatives were made of glass; making prints was complicated, time-consuming work. But by the early 1900s, the invention of the dry-plate negative, hand-held cameras, and eventually flexible film that could be sent out for developing changed the nature of photography. The camera was no longer "an exotic instrument." Amateurs photographed their family, friends, vacations, pets, and backyards. They experimented with techniques, poses, and points of view. Professional photographers were also influenced by these changes and used the new, lighter-weight equipment to venture away from the studio and record scenes of everyday life. Their compositions became more spontaneous and informal. They could more easily record action and take photographs under less than ideal conditions.

The large number of photographs produced as a result of these changes helped to create a visual culture in the United States. After 1900 readers began to expect to see timely and dramatic photographs accompanying stories in newspapers and magazines. Businesses increasingly used photographs to sell goods and services. In 1901, the *New*

York Times won the praise of its peers because "it does not print pictures." However, in 1904, the *Times* bowing to readers' expectations, began using photographs to illustrate news stories, and the next year it reintroduced its *Sunday Magazine* as a photographic pictorial. Camera sales, especially after Kodak introduced its $1 Brownie camera in 1900, climbed dramatically. Camera clubs, magazines, and exhibitions flourished in the 1920s and 1930s. In 1936 the first issue of *Life*, the popular magazine devoted to photojournalism appeared. That same year writer James Agee called the camera "the central instrument of our time."

Coincidentally, photography's rapid development paralleled a vast expansion of Federal Government power. In 1880 there were 95,000 civilian employees working for the Federal Government, most of them postal employees. By 1900 there were 230,000 Federal workers, and by 1917 that number had almost doubled. Federal spending also grew. In 1914 the Federal Government spent about $1 billion. That number had jumped to more than $3½ billion in 1922, grew to over $9 billion in 1936, and topped $100 billion in 1944. The latter jump, of course, was due primarily to war spending. Growth could be seen on an agency level, as well. In 1899, for example, the Office of the Supervising Architect, the design and construction arm of the U.S. Treasury Department, managed 399 projects. In 1912 they were managing 1,126.

But these statistical increases are only one way to measure Federal influence on American life. Even by the early years of the century, the advent of new Federal agencies that sought to regulate, encourage, enlighten, build, or investigate made the Government more involved in people's lives than it ever had been before. During the Great Depression, the New Deal fashioned a more activist role for the state as an economic regulator and as a provider of economic security. Two world wars not only increased cooperation among business, Government, and labor but also created mechanisms for military conscription, propaganda, and internal security. The Cold War gave birth to what President Dwight Eisenhower labeled "a military-industrial complex," and forced issues of national security, civil defense, and "un-American activities" into everyday discussion. The Great Society programs and environmental legislation of the late 1960s and 1970s further deepened the Nation's reliance on Federal problem solving. By mid-century, when Americans spoke of "the government," either to praise or damn it, they usually meant the Federal Government.

The intersection of these two 20th-century trends—the growing popularity of photography and the expansion of Federal power—provide a starting point for understanding the images reproduced in this book. Most were taken by photographers working for the Federal Government. Those that were not taken by Government employees or contractors were either collected by a Federal agency or became part of the Federal record through the legislative process, a Federal investigation, or a court case. These photographic prints, negatives, lantern slides, color slides, transparencies, and other assorted images have now become part of the National Archives of the United States, which is administered by the National Archives and Records Administration (NARA).

NARA is the Federal agency given the task of receiving, caring for, and making available the historic records of the U.S. Government. By any measure, its photography holdings are vast. In the Washington, DC, area alone, they consist of more than 8 million photographs in the still picture stacks, 9 million aerial photographs among cartographic records. In addition, tens of thousands more photographs are filed with NARA's billions of textual records such as the letters, memos, and reports, legislative records, or Federal court case files preserved in Washington, DC, and around the country.

The numbers are imposing even when they are broken down into smaller units. National Archives holdings are organized into "record groups" relating to the particular agency, bureau, or commission that created and used the records. Each group is assigned a number. Record Group (RG) 111, for example, is the Records of the Office of the Chief Signal Officer. The Signal Corps was the U.S. Army's unit in charge of, among other things, recording Army operations in photographs. At last count there were 1,348,662 images in the Signal Corps photography holdings at the National Archives at College Park, Maryland. These images cover the history of the U.S. Army and include everything from photographs of artwork depicting the American Revolution to color photos of the Vietnam War. Another military-related record group, RG 373, Records of the Defense Intelligence Agency, contains more than 6 million aerial photographs of the United States and foreign areas. Held among cartographic records at College Park because of their close connection to mapping, these photographs include World War II aerial photography of the Normandy and Iwo Jima landings, captured German and Japanese aerials, and satellite imagery from the 1960s and early 1970s.

Elsewhere in NARA, the numbers are similarly large. The Nation's first federally managed Presidential library, the Franklin D. Roosevelt Library, contains approximately

130,000 photographs documenting the lives of President and Eleanor Roosevelt, including the 12 years FDR was President. As testament to the growth of photographic coverage of Presidents and their families, one of the most recent Presidential libraries, the Ronald Reagan Library boasts more than 1.5 million photographs of Ronald and Nancy Reagan both before and during their 8 years as President and First Lady.

It is easy to see how a researcher could be overwhelmed by these numbers, but with a bit of persistence (and the assistance of an archivist), researchers will uncover wonderful 20th-century gems among the mountains of photographs at the National Archives. Some of these were taken by famous photographers. For example, among the 59,864 images in RG 79, Records of the National Park Service, are 226 original signed Ansel Adams prints of the American West (figs. 86–89). In RG 83, Records of the Bureau of Agricultural Economics (26,000 images), are photographs by Dorothea Lange depicting the devastating impact of the Great Depression on migrant farm families (figs. 81–83, 85). The collections of the Presidential libraries contain images by photographers such as David Hume Kennerly (fig. 150) and Yoichi Okamoto (figs. 130–133). Their photographs give rare glimpses into White House life and provide unique insight into world-changing events such as the assassination of President John F. Kennedy, the resignation of President Richard Nixon, and policy making during the Persian Gulf War.

Other NARA photographs were taken by individuals about whom we know little or nothing. In the regional records facility in Anchorage, Alaska, for example, are hundreds of prints depicting the lives of Native Alaskans in the early 1900s. Federal court case files in the regions hold photographs that were submitted as evidence in a variety of disputes. Many photographs in the massive military record groups at the College Park facility are linked to the names of soldiers, sailors, or marines who found themselves working as photographers, sometimes in extraordinary situations, but who never became famous even though their photographs may have.

Why did the Federal Government produce and collect such huge numbers of photographs over the last 100 years? What messages did it want to convey? The answers to these questions are unique to the image being considered, but a few generalizations can be made. Many Federal photographs have what photohistorian James Guimond identifies as an "informational" purpose. They describe how a piece of machinery might have looked, how high a crop had grown, or what varieties of plant, fruit, or nut grew in a particular climate, and they communicate this factual information to us in a "deliberately neutral" fashion. These images can tell us much about the details of a particular scene or time. They can also be well composed and show great technical skill, but they are not usually compelling.

Not all "official images," however, were merely informational, and some Government photographers did not see themselves as neutral observers. Several agencies funded large documentary photography projects during the century. While these projects were often promoted as purely descriptive, in reality they promoted an agency or Governmental agenda. Dependent on Congress for funding, the President for direction, and the public for support, Federal agencies had a great stake in documenting successful or even failed programs. Throughout the century, photography was one tool agencies used to demonstrate how they carried out their missions. During wartime, Government photography sometimes went even further, crossing the boundary between advocacy and propaganda.

Also implicit in many Government photos is the interaction between the Government and the photographer. Federal photographers had varying amounts of freedom with  which to approach their work. Agencies could be very specific about their assignments, but they could also give photog- raphers a great deal of leeway about subjects or composition. A pho- tographer working for the Agriculture Depart- ment in the 1930s, for example, might be given broad topics such as "Farm Engineering" or "Health and Community Cooperation," or he might be asked to shoot more specific subjects such as images of "negro women making quilts and mat- tresses." On rare occa- sions, agencies might provide their photogra- phers with "scripts," out- lines of subjects that would be of interest. But even in these few cases, most details, including the exact framing, timing, angle of view, and who was going to be photographed in which poses, was left to the photographer's discretion. Unfortunately, the background materials—the letters, memorandums, and other directions to photographers—that might have helped us understand agency or individual intentions have not always survived along with the images. This is especially true of photographs from the early decades of the century.

How then do we begin to "read" a historical photograph and decipher its broader meaning? What obstacles stop us and what resources assist us along the way? The first step, one that takes little formal training, is to simply examine, study, and enjoy the image. After that, several questions come to mind. What is the central focus of the photograph? What details strike you as important? Was it taken from an unusual angle or distance? What are the people wearing? What are their facial expressions? How are they gesturing? Who or what is included in the image and who or what might be missing?

Next, examine any available caption information. What is the date and location of the photograph? Who is the photographer? Is there a narrative caption as well as basic descriptive information? Comparing and contrasting images can also prove useful. Fully answering these questions might require historical research, which might or might not shed light on the image. What do we know about the location and date of the photograph? How might the image illustrate a particular historical event or trend? What do we know about the photographer and his or her work?

Finally, "reading" photographs demands an appreciation and acknowledgment of a photohistorian's own cultural, social, and political assumptions. While it is crucial to find and evaluate whatever external evidence exists about an image, it is just as important to understand that in the end, photographic interpretation (like all historical interpretation) is subjective. Two people evaluating the same evidence will view an image through differing sets of perspectives, and each might reach radically dissimilar conclusions about a photograph's meaning and importance. While this subjectivity has its dangers, it also promotes a creative dialogue. In the words of photographer Rondal Partridge, "You ask questions of great photographs, and great photographs ask questions of you." Over the following pages, we will examine a few of the NARA images in "Picturing the Century," put them in historical context, and provide background about how the Federal Government used them. Hopefully, we will also engage in a creative dialogue with these images and their makers and raise important questions about 20th-century America.

A New Century

New Year's Day 1900 found Americans celebrating but also struggling with change. Within a few decades, the United States had rapidly transformed from a largely agrarian Nation of rural hamlets to an industrial giant whose citizens lived increasingly in cities. The Nation's population was growing, especially from an influx of immigrants—more than 425,000 in 1900 alone. There were many reasons for Americans to be optimistic. Their Nation was becoming a world power. Technological innovations—the telephone, the automobile, the electric lightbulb, and after 1903, the airplane—promised to make life easier and more enjoyable. Medical progress and better nutrition were lowering infant mortality rates and raising life expectancy. But there were disturbing trends, as well. Although the Nation was founded on ideals of equality and opportunity, American society exhibited great differences in wealth and influence. Cities were symbols of progress, but they were also hubs of poverty. America's growing industrial output brought higher wages but also long hours and difficult working conditions for its laborers. Millions could not vote because of their race, economic status, ethnicity, or gender.

Four NARA photographs of street scenes from four very different places in the early 20th century serve as good starting points for investigating these issues. The first shows New York City's Fifth Avenue on Easter Morning, 1900 (fig. 11). This is clearly a fashionable section of the city. Well-to-do crowds dressed in their Easter finery parade down the sidewalks, observing the social conventions of the upper classes. Streets are paved and filled with elegant horse-drawn carriages. The automobile is still uncommon: Only one is visible. Large mansions, some still under construction, have been built on either side of the avenue. We can see only a few faces, but those that we do see are white.

Just a few miles away, in another section of New York City, we find a much different street. This is Hester Street in the largely immigrant section of New York's Lower East Side (fig. 12). Hester Street in 1903, like Fifth Avenue in 1900, is teeming with activity, but this time the subjects are street vendors, peddlers, and customers. Signs are in Yiddish as well as English. There is no clear differentiation between living and business spaces. The buildings on Hester Street serve as both shops and tenements where extended families might be living in small, crowded apartments. The faces on Hester Street are different, too. Those pictured appear to come primarily from Eastern or Southern Europe. Their dress seems to retain a European look. Most have probably been in the United States for only a short time.

We find our third street a continent away from New York City. "Steadman Ave., Nome, Alaska" (fig. 13) was located in a classic "boomtown" in the extreme western part of the Territory. In 1898, gold had been discovered in nearby Anvil Creek, and over the next few months, 20,000 prospectors, miners, saloonkeepers, surveyors, and prostitutes found their way to Nome. In the photo, Steadman Avenue is unpaved and narrow; its buildings have only been in existence a few months. All the figures in the photo are white men. Hastily erected signs, advertising everything from cigars and liquor to lawyers and mining investments, fill the streets. Both the town and the townspeople have a raw, rough, and unfinished appearance.

The fourth photograph comes from Seattle, Washington. It shows a "street" at the 1909 Alaskan Yukon Pacific Exposition (fig. 9). The exposition was one of a series of dazzling fairs and expositions held around the Nation from the 1890s through the early 20th century. These fairs celebrated America's technological and social progress and were showcases not only for inventions, machinery, and agricultural improvements but also for the architects who designed the fairgrounds as temporary fantasy "cities" with stately boulevards, lakes, statues, and courtyards. Pictured in the photograph are the entrance arches, large monumental structures, welcoming the public to what is a special, celebratory event.

While no four photographs can possibly comprehensively cover early-20th-century America, with some historical research, these National Archives photographs can be shown to illustrate several of the major trends of those years. Around 1900 the United States was quickly becoming an urban nation. It had much to celebrate, but it was also a Nation that had sharp distinctions of class and ethnicity. There was also tremendous geographic diversity. Even in the midst of an urban transformation, there were isolated, undeveloped places. The photographs also allow the reader to compare dress, housing, social customs, and transportation.

After examining the obvious visual clues, however, many questions remain, and research in NARA files can sometimes add to the stock of information. For instance, who took the four photographs? In each case the photographer is described as "unknown." When were they taken? For some, we have exact dates; for others, we have only approximate dates. Why did these images end up in agency files? We know, for example, that the photographs of Fifth Avenue and the Alaskan Yukon Pacific Exposition were found in the files of the Bureau of Roads. That might generally explain the interest in New York City traffic, but it is of little help with the Seattle exposition photograph. The Nome, Alaska photograph is found among other images of Alaska in Signal Corps files, but there is no indication as to why the Army needed to document Steadman Avenue, Nome, or the gold rush. We have a little more information regarding the Hester Street photograph. It is filed among the records of the Public Housing Administration in a series of photographs, many of them lantern slides, collected in 1937 to document "low income housing."

Many other early-20th-century images lack clear documentation of their intentions. A 1900 Signal Corps photograph, for example, shows "Troop L, 6th Cavalry" posed between two life-size stone elephants on the "Avenue of Statues, near Ming Tombs, Near Pekin (*sic*)" (fig. 10). The photograph was taken by Capt. Cornelius Francis O'Keefe, a photographer assigned to the Army Corps of Engineers to photograph some of the activities of the 2,500 U.S. troops taking part in the China Relief Expedition. The expedition had been sent to China in the wake of the Boxer Rebellion, during which a group of Chinese nationalists, known in the West as the Boxers, had laid siege to foreign embassies in Beijing. But why did O'Keefe choose to pose these troops in this particular way? Why, for example, did he place an American military unit in between two ancient Chinese elephants? Was he simply marking that Troop L had been in China? Was he using an old photographic trick to give the viewer a sense of scale? Or was he, perhaps even unconsciously, making a visual statement about the United States emerging as a player in world politics by sending its military abroad?

Other early-20th-century images were taken or collected to record important "firsts," such as the first powered flight (fig. 16), the first park rangers in Yosemite National Park (fig. 14), or the early use of an assembly line (fig. 17). Photos also documented tragedies such as the San Francisco earthquake of 1906 (fig. 27) and the Seward, Alaska flood of 1917 (fig. 28). The photographs of Walter Lubken (figs. 30–34), taken for the Bureau of Reclamation, document the agency's dam and canal building projects around the American West. The Bureau hoped Lubken's images of the towns near the projects would stimulate interest among potential settlers and demonstrate how irrigation could turn desert into fertile farmland. They also represent an updated version of the American myth that western settlement provided unlimited opportunities for those willing to work hard and take a chance.

Photographs were sometimes taken for inclusion in a report or investigation. Despite the beaming face of one of the shopkeepers behind the counter at the Washington, DC, Center Market (fig. 24), this photo was taken to demonstrate unsanitary conditions in the market, especially the uncovered food displayed

PAMPHLET No. 213

National Child Labor Committee
INCORPORATED
105 EAST 22D STREET
NEW YORK CITY

CHILD LABOR AT THE NATIONAL CAPITAL

IN THE SHADOW OF THE DOME.

Eight-, nine-, ten- and eleven-year-old newsboys selling papers in violation of the law

By A. J. McKELWAY.
Secretary for the Southern States, National Child Labor Committee, 204 Bond Bldg., Washington, D. C.

Photographs by
LEWIS W. HINE, Staff Photographer

1 **Child Labor at the National Capital**
By A.J. McKelway, 1913
Photographs by Lewis Hine
National Archives and Records Administration,
Records of the U.S. House of Representatives
Reproduced with permission of the U.S. House
of Representatives

there. A case file in the Immigration and Naturalization Service records holds the striking photograph of Lee Wai She and her children (fig. 22). Lee Wai She submitted the photograph as partial evidence in her successful effort to prove the Hawaiian birth of her children. Such proof was necessary in order to establish their right to stay in the United States under the Chinese Exclusion Act, which prohibited the immigration of Chinese nationals. The files of the Commission on Industrial Relations contain a photograph of a funeral for victims of the 1914 "Ludlow Massacre," in which 21 people died after the Colorado State militia attacked a tent colony of striking coal miners and their families (fig. 29).

Also during the first part of the century, organizations such as the National Child Labor Committee (NCLC) used Lewis Hine's photographs, documenting child labor across the

7

United States (fig. 35), to lobby Congress and state legislatures to pass laws restricting the employment of children under specified ages. The NCLC pioneered the use of pamphlets, posters, leaflets, and mass mailings to gain support for their position. Hine traveled the country photographing a variety of industries and making notes on children's ages, heights, and stories. A few of these photos were used in a NCLC pamphlet supporting legislation to restrict the use of children as messengers, peddlers, and shoeshiners in Washington, DC. When the House of Representatives considered this legislation, members used the pamphlet and Hine's prints to document these labor practices. Other Hine child-labor photographs fell into Government hands when he gave hundreds of his prints to the Labor Department's Children's Bureau after it was established in 1912.

More typical of how photographs came to NARA are the images of immigrants arriving at Ellis Island in the early years of the century (figs. 20–21). They are found among the records of the Public Health Service that make up the agency's master photograph file. For the most part, these images document advances in public health and sanitation, such as fumigation, hygiene education, and scientific research on communicable diseases. As immigration to the United States increased at the end of the 19th and beginning of the 20th centuries, the Public Health Service (USPHS) became responsible for screening new arrivals to the country for infectious diseases. Since Ellis Island was the principal point of entry for immigrants on the east coast, the immigration station there was covered extensively. Many of the photographs in this series document examination procedures and screening techniques used by USPHS personnel, but these photos also capture the dreams and fears of the immigrants in their nervous faces.

The Great War & the New Era

In April 1917 the United States entered World War I, or the Great War as it was then called, against Germany and Austria-Hungary. The Federal Government immediately mobilized American society to meet the demands of "total war." Millions volunteered for or were drafted into military service. The Government worked with business, labor, and agriculture to increase weapon and food production. War also quickened the pace of social change. Black Americans moved to industrial cities to work in war industries and also served in the Armed Forces in unprecedented numbers. Mobilization placed women in jobs previously closed to them and helped bring the fight for woman suffrage to a successful conclusion.

Federal agencies mobilized public opinion by using photography to "sell the war." Images taken by Government photographers or collected from commercial sources were used to convince Americans that the war was just, to stir patriotic fervor, and to record for history the actions of the military and other wartime agencies. Along with other public relations devices such as posters, silent movies, rallies, music, parades, and pamphlets, the Government used photographs to foster a sense of community participation, to encourage sacrifice, and to convey a sense of excitement about the war effort. The war, wrote William Gibbs MacAdoo, President Woodrow Wilson's Treasury Secretary, was "a crusade, and like all crusades, it sweeps along on a powerful stream of romanticism." Tapping this emotion meant going "directly to the people" and exploiting "the profound impulse called patriotism."

Photographs of Liberty Bond rallies illustrate how these techniques worked. The bonds, which were a tool used by the Government to finance the war, were sold at rallies often attended by hundreds, even thousands of citizens. The crowds would be addressed by "Four Minute Men," who would give short, intense speeches urging the crowd to subscribe to the bond issue. Silent movie stars such as Mary Pickford, "Fatty" Arbuckle, and Douglas Fairbanks toured the country promoting bonds. Of course, these events were also accompanied by singing, flag-waving, and other forms of patriotic hoopla (fig. 40). While they were usually aimed at civilians, these patriotic extravaganzas also made use of those

in uniform. A customary practice at such rallies was the making of giant photographic tableaus. Photographers, with the aid of a panoramic camera, would photograph at a distance large numbers of soldiers positioned into various inspiring shapes such as shields, the flag, or the Statue of Liberty. The "Liberty Day Celebration" at Camp Grant in Illinois (fig. 43) shows one such photograph in progress. The photographer has climbed atop a flag-draped speaker's platform with his large camera. Stretching out in front of him is a phalanx of hundreds of soldiers. The image also unintentionally catches a less noble aspect of World War I military life: The units in the photograph were racially segregated.

Another tableau (fig. 48), this one in a drugstore window in Maquoketa, Iowa, supported food conservation. The centerpiece of the display was a "corps" of potatoes mounted on blocks to look like soldiers. One of these "potatriots" is former President Teddy Roosevelt; another appears to be President Wilson. The display urges citizens on with slogans such as "Join the Ranks and Spud the Kaiser" and "The potato is a good soldier. Eat it uniform and all." The pharmacy also offered free recipes for using potatoes in place of wheat, which the Government was attempting to conserve. This photo is part of the records of the U.S. Food Administration, a war-time agency headed by Herbert Hoover that attempted to regulate the supply, distribution, and consumption of food during the war.

In 1917 the Government, for the first time since the Civil War, drafted men into the military. Fears that conscription would mean a repeat of the draft riots that plagued Northern cities during the Civil War proved unfounded. On June 5, 1917, almost 10 million men enthusiastically registered for the draft. Eventually, 2.8 million were conscripted, and another 2 million volunteered. By the summer of 1918, nearly 10,000 troops left for France each day. Photographs of these departures were posed to play upon the emotions and promote patriotic service. When the "Fighting 69th" Infantry Regiment left New York City before sailing for France (fig. 41), the men were "bid a fond goodbye" by flag-waving "sweethearts," who kissed them passionately. Such images fostered the view that local communities (except for a few conscientious objectors and radicals here and there) enthusiastically backed military service for their men and that the men going off to war had the unwavering support of the Nation.

Once in France, the American Expeditionary Force (AEF), as the U.S. Army and Marine units were called, were put into combat slowly. While the AEF grew and received further training, the untested American troops defended a quiet sector of the front. They eventually fought in several major engagements, beginning in the spring of 1918, but overall suffered far fewer casualties than other belligerent nations. War in the trenches of France was a particularly horrible experience, but military photographers, who had to deal with large bulky equipment, found it difficult to record the grisly face of battle. While many NARA Signal Corps and War Department images show the destructiveness of trench warfare, battle-weary American troops, and support activities, few photographers were able to record combat. Some of the most poignant images are those of the wounded. The grim portrait of a badly wounded soldier with those caring for him at an American hospital in France (fig. 42) makes for one of the more candid views of the results of war.

Photographers also caught many aspects of the industrial as well as the military mobilization. Within NARA's holdings are images of aircraft, munitions, and ordnance manufacturing, but photographs of shipbuilding are especially numerous. As German submarine attacks on merchant shipping threatened to reduce supplies sent to France, it became especially critical that U.S. shipyards produce merchant vessels to replace those sunk by the Germans and to build Navy ships to protect transports on their voyages across the Atlantic. Shipbuilding was so important to the war effort that the Government set up the Emergency Fleet Corporation (EFC) to speed construction. Considering the late date, the EFC built a surprising number of wooden-hulled ships. One panoramic photograph of the Grant-Smith-Porter Company shipyards in Aberdeen, Washington, shows its workers in front of several of the partially constructed wooden ships (fig. 44).

The wartime mobilization of American society had several unexpected consequences. One was the presence of African American men in the military. African Americans had served in segregated units in the military for many years, but the prospect of their being drafted in large numbers frightened segregationists, especially after racial violence involving black soldiers broke out in Houston, Texas, in 1917. After struggling with questions as to where would black units be trained, who would command them, and how would they be utilized, the War Department created two black combat divisions. Once in France—despite poor equipment, little training, and efforts to assign them to manual labor—four regiments of the 93d Division were placed under French command and fought at the battles of Argonne, Château-Thierry, and Belleau Wood. The 369th Infantry Regiment spent 191 consecutive days at the front. Several of its members (fig. 46) won individual decorations, and the entire 369th won the Croix de Guerre for their bravery. Secretary of War Newton Baker called the unit the all-round most serviceable regiment sent to France.

In another unexpected development, as more men were drafted or volunteered for the military, women began to take their places in the workforce. About 1 million women held wartime jobs, many of which were traditionally male. Some, like the integrated group of "rivet heaters and passers on" working at the U.S. Navy yard along the Puget Sound in Washington (fig. 47), worked in heavy industry. Others worked as railway conductors, telegraph and mail deliverers, nurses, or telephone operators. The photography files from the Women's Bureau records exaggerate the progress made by working women during the war by emphasizing the novelty of women working, for example, as the first two "girl ushers" used at a Chicago baseball stadium in July 1918 (fig. 50). While some fields showed permanent increases in female workers after the war, for the most part women were simply temporarily moving up from lower-paying jobs. Despite misconceptions about the number of women working before the war, few women were new to the workforce.

World War I also created expectations in many American women that their patriotic service would be rewarded with the right to vote. The largest suffrage organization, the National American Woman Suffrage Association (NAWSA) headed by Carrie Chapman

Catt, threw its weight behind American participation, aligned itself with President Woodrow Wilson politically, and lobbied Congress behind the scenes for the vote. In 1918, Wilson rewarded this support by telling the Senate that suffrage was "vital to the winning the war" and urging Congress to pass a Constitutional amendment granting women the right to vote.

Not all suffrage organizations, however, followed NAWSA's lead. Other more militant suffrage groups, notably the National Woman's Party led by Alice Paul, refused to support the war and used tactics such as street protests and hunger strikes to further the cause. Some of these women took their protest directly to the White House where in 1918 one stood with a banner charging the President with hypocrisy for talking of self-determination while "20,000,000 American women are not self-governed" (fig. 51). Eventually, the combined pressure of both approaches led to the passage of the 19th amendment guaranteeing the vote to women.

Victory on the battlefields of France, it was hoped, was to be followed by what some called an affluent "New Era." And in many ways the 1920s were truly new. For the first time, more people lived in cities than on farms. Prosperity, technological innovation, and advertising created the world's first mass-consumption economy. Consumer goods such as radios, automobiles, washing machines, and refrigerators became affordable; sports and movies became big business; businessmen and inventors became celebrities. The decade was also a time of profound social tensions between the traditionally minded, rural, old-stock Americans and the newer, immigrant, city dwellers. Issues such as prohibition, immigration restriction, and the growth of the Ku Klux Klan epitomized these strains.

The armistice that ended the fighting in November 1918 brought with it a rapid demobilization. The Federal Government canceled war-related contracts, emergency agencies quickly went out of business, and the military released men back into civilian life. One casualty of the rapid demobilization was the Federal Government's ability to record its activities photographically. As wartime agencies closed down, their photographers either left Government service or returned to their prewar jobs. Many of the larger established bureaus continued to employ photographers but with smaller staffs. As a result, many of the National Archives images of 1920s America come from the courts or are culled from newspaper or commercial sources. An example of this non-Governmental material is the photo morgue of *The New York Times* Paris Bureau. The collection, which covers a period from 1900 to ca. 1950, is an especially strong resource for the years between World Wars I and II. It was purchased by the Government and then transferred to several bureaus before becoming a part of the United States Information Agency files in 1954.

Interestingly, for a nation that was now predominantly urban, some of the most active agency photography programs during the 1920s concentrated their efforts on agriculture. Organizations such as the Bureau of Agricultural Economics (BAE) and the Extension Service carried out widespread coverage of farm life. BAE photographs centered on developments in marketing and standardization of agricultural products and the establishment of agricultural cooperatives, but they also demonstrate the changes that were coming to rural America during the 1920s. These included improved transportation, health care (fig. 49), and education. Likewise, the photographs of longtime Extension Service photographer George Ackerman (figs. 59–63) highlighted progressive, up-to-date farmers who used the latest labor-saving devices and enjoyed the benefits of modern conveniences in their homes.

The Government also took care to record significant developments in several other fields. For example, when Congress established a Federal Board of Vocational Education to provide vocational rehabilitation to veterans, it also created a system of grants-in-aid to state universities that would administer these training programs. During the 1920s the Board photographed examples of training classes and trainees who were completing their courses of study (fig. 53). The Post Office Department publicized the growth of airmail service, tracing its development with pictures of airplanes, hangars, repair crews, and pilots. One of these ostensibly showed the winter flying clothing of U.S. Mail Service pilot William C. Hopson (fig. 54), but it also showcases Hopson's virile handsomeness and gave a sense of the celebrity status of flyers in the 1920s and 1930s.

During the 1920s the Immigration and Naturalization Service (INS) continued to add to its already voluminous case files on Chinese immigrants. Poverty and political turmoil in China as well as eco-  nomic opportunity in the United States during the late 19th century led many Chinese to come to this country. However, after 1882, Chinese were barred from entering the country under the Chi- nese Exclusion Act which allowed only four cat- egories of exemptions: merchants, students, mis- sionaries, and diplomats (and their immediate families). Those claiming an exemption had to obtain a certificate as proof of their right to be in the country, and many individuals wanting to come to the United States resorted to buying false documents which purported the bearers were the children or wives of legal immigrants.

In an effort to stop this illegal immigration, the INS investigated each exemption claim. In 1926, when 16-year-old Wong Yuey Ock applied to enter the country, he claimed to be a merchant's son. His declaration sparked an INS investigation into his alleged father's business. The resulting file includes several photographs of the merchant's store (fig. 57). Since the store's stock was valued at only $300 and because a fan tan game was under way in a room adjacent to the store, the investigator concluded that Wong's "father" was chiefly a gambler. He also found discrepancies in the two men's descriptions of their native village. Wong Yuey Ock was eventually deported.

Such investigations were only one sign of nativism in America. A more dangerous form of this anti-immigrant sentiment could be seen in the rebirth of the Ku Klux Klan. This violently anti-black, anti-Semitic, anti-Catholic, anti-union, and anti-immigrant secret society grew from about 200,000 to 2 million between 1920 and 1925. Once confined to the rural South, where it had originated after the Civil War, the Klan now grew fastest in the Middle West, the Southwest, and cities. In Oregon a politician backed by the Klan won the governorship; in Oklahoma the Klan helped impeach the governor; in Indiana it controlled both houses of the legislature and both U.S. Senators. Profoundly fascistic in its philosophy, the Klan used terror and violence to intimidate minority groups and those who opposed it. Its secret rituals, mysterious robes and hoods, and prejudicial rhetoric looked back, as the Klan claimed, to a "golden past" before America had been "corrupted," but the organization also used modern symbols, such as when two aviator Klansmen in Dayton, Ohio, thrilled a gathering of their brothers in 1924 with a display of daring airmanship (fig. 52).

A Kansas City, Missouri, court case brought another 1920s image to the National Archives. When the Royal Picture Theater erected electric signs and a large canopy in front of its entrance as advertising, the neighboring Robinson Shoe Store objected, claiming the display blocked shoppers' view of their establishment. A lawsuit followed, and the court ordered photographs taken that showed a number of views of the theater. One of these is of the theater's large marquee promoting the 1927 silent film *It* (fig. 55). Coincidentally, the photo also illustrates such aspects of life in the 1920s as increasing urbanization, the popularization of the automobile, the growth of mass entertainment, and the proliferation of advertising. It also depicts the emergence of the modern woman. *It*, the movie being advertised, starred Clara Bow, who became known as the archetypal wild and flirtatious "flapper girl" of the 1920s. In popular usage to have "It" was to have sex appeal, and Bow naturally became the "It" Girl.

Movie stardom was only one form of celebrity in the 1920s. The growth of spectator sports brought athletes such as Babe Ruth (baseball), Jack Dempsey (boxing), "Red" Grange (football), and Bobby Jones (golf) public acclaim. Record-breaking aviator Charles Lindbergh was probably the most well-known man in America after his solo flight across the Atlantic Ocean in 1927. But celebrities also came from the worlds of business (Henry Ford), music (Rudy Vallee), and science (Thomas Edison). One often overlooked hero of the period was Herbert Hoover (fig. 56). Too often remembered as the inflexible and uncaring President during the Great Depression, Hoover was hailed in the 1920s for leading humanitarian efforts during and after World War I and for his advocacy of efficiency and rationality in economic planning during his service as Secretary of Commerce under Presidents Warren Harding and Calvin Coolidge. When President Hoover joined Ford and business tycoon Harvey Firestone in 1929 to honor Edison on his 82d birthday, the occasion was seen as a gathering of four of the leading luminaries of the decade.

The Great Depression & the New Deal

The prosperity of the 1920s ended with an economic catastrophe of unequaled length and severity—the Great Depression. By 1933 industrial production had fallen to one-third its pre-Depression level, thousands of banks had closed, and almost 13 million Americans were jobless. In cities, soup kitchens were commonplace, and in the countryside, crops rotted because farmers were unable to sell them. To make matters worse, in 1930 and 1931 a devastating drought struck parts of the South and Midwest, and its effects lingered on into the mid-1930s. While President Hoover's attempts at combating the economic disaster were far more extensive than those taken by any previous Chief Executive, he refused to do more. Consequently, as the crisis deepened, the public began to blame the President. In 1932 he lost a landslide election to New York Governor Franklin D. Roosevelt, who pledged a "New Deal" for the American people.

The New Deal aimed at promoting economic recovery and putting Americans back to work through increased Federal activism. New laws regulated banking and the stock market. New Federal agencies attempted to control agricultural production, stabilize wages and prices, and create a vast public works program for the unemployed. These initiatives did not end the Great Depression, but they did correct many failings in the economic system and alleviate much suffering.

Many of the New Deal-era Government agencies also sponsored photography projects. For the most part, these projects used a "documentary" approach that emphasized straightforward views and concentrated on scenes of everyday life or the environment. The projects touted the social achievements of the New Deal or pointed out the need for further Government reforms. Many notable 20th-century American photographers—including Dorothea Lange, Walker Evans, Jack Delano, Russell Lee, Marion Post Wolcott, and Arthur Rothstein—worked for one or more of the Government photography projects. The projects and their World War II successors also opened doors for women and minorities seeking careers in photography. Taken together, these New Deal images make for a detailed portrait of America during the 1930s and early 1940s.

The most famous of these projects was undertaken by the Resettlement Administration, later renamed the Farm Security Administration (FSA) which was led by Roy Stryker. The thousands of negatives and prints produced by the FSA now reside in the Library of Congress, but there was no shortage of creative photography outside of the FSA. The Works Progress Administration (WPA), the Bureau of Agricultural Economic (BEA), the Civilian Conservation Corps (CCC), the National Youth Administration (NYA), the Public Works Administration (PWA), and the Rural Electrification Administration (REA) all sponsored smaller photography programs that helped make the 1930s and early 1940s a golden age of documentary photography. Many of the photographs made by the men and women working for these agencies, as well as some taken by photographers outside the Government, are now held by the National Archives.

The Depression created many opportunities for photographers to record the effects of the economic crisis and the social conflict it engendered. Some photographers chose to concentrate on the hardships the Depression had brought to individuals. The most well-known of these was Dorothea Lange, whose work for the FSA and later the BAE, put a human face on the Depression. Lange's photographs (figs. 81–85), especially those of migrant workers, are often filled with hopelessness and poverty, yet Lange still managed to maintain her subjects' dignity and individuality. The photographers Arnold Eagle and David Robbins examined the urban poverty of the Depression in their photographic series entitled "One-Third of a Nation." One of the photos from the series (fig. 66) shows an all-too-common sight during the Depression—an elderly woman forced by poverty to sell pencils on the street. Eagle and Robbins intensified the emotional impact of the photo by juxtaposing the woman with a storefront display of the latest spring fashions.

The decade's social conflict also received coverage. An example from 1932 is a photograph of police battling with members of the so-called "bonus army," a group of veterans who had come to Washington, DC, to demand that Congress give them their military pension bonuses early. When Congress did not act, the protesters, most of whom had nowhere else to go, set up camp in Anacostia, a section of Washington, DC. They remained there for several months. After a series of violent confrontations with the police, the "army" was eventually driven out of the city by Federal troops and its shanty town destroyed. The photograph, taken by an Associated Press staffer, shows the violence of the moment, but it also goes beyond simply recording the scene. The notion that those who had fought for their country were now forced to fight with police in the Nation's Capital raised questions about the state of the Republic. The center of the photo, showing a protester and policeman struggling over an American flag, is especially fraught with symbolism (fig. 68). Sheldon Dick's photograph of a United Auto Workers' sitdown strike (fig. 67) is another example of Federal photography catching social change. Dick's photograph uses a humorous touch to convey the determination and power of the strikers, who seized the General Motors plant in Flint, Michigan for 6 weeks in January and February 1937. The image of the strikers as they sat reading on the very car seats they usually made reinforces the idea that these men were in the struggle for the long run and that they, not the corporation, were in control of the plant's operations.

But if there are good examples of photographs of hard times and unrest, there are many more New Deal photographs that capture the benign and commonplace aspects of American life. These scenes of everyday life may not have been as politically charged as some of the more strident images of poverty and conflict, but they provide us with a window into the change and continuity of 20th-century America. Often these are street scenes, shots of family life, or photographs of recreational activities. For example, two unknown photographers recorded scenes on two streets in New York City. One from the files of the National Youth Administration (fig. 73) shows a "Street Corner Next to Federal Building where the U.S. Dept. Of Labor handles naturalization of immigrants." Another shows Harlem's shopping district (fig. 79). Both capture the feel of daily life through compositions that emphasize signs, businesses, and people going about their daily routines.

Other photos depict smalltown life. Two by BAE photographer Irving Rusinow were designed to be included in the Bureau's comparative studies of rural communities. The first (fig. 70), taken in 1941 in a town in Shelby County in Southwest Iowa, shows the town's poolhall, one of two examples of the coming of "commercialized entertainment in the village." While Rusinow's image is quaint to our eyes, his caption emphasized how more individuals were turning to this type of entertainment despite the disapproval of the town's "most substantial citizens" to such establishments. A second Rusinow image, taken in El Cerrito, New Mexico for another of the community studies, shows the home of an American of Hispanic ancestry (fig. 72). Not only does the image give us an impression of the subject's great bearing and dignity, but it also allows us to see the trappings of his life: the wood stove that dominates the photograph's foreground, the religious icons on the wall, a bed, a dresser, and a trunk.

Celebrating the social and economic progress made under President Roosevelt (fig. 77) was another important theme in New Deal photography. Federal photographers emphasized what the Nation had gained under Roosevelt and publicized his administration's achievements. These photographs tended to be of two types. The first chronicled the large public works projects undertaken by the Government. These might show, for example, the massive turbines that generated electricity at the Tennessee Valley Authority's Pickwick Dam (fig. 71). Or they might picture the progress of the construction of the Boulder Dam (fig. 64). Photographs like these typically tried to give some sense of the scale and impressiveness of these projects, often expressing size placing a figure dwarfed by machinery nearby. While New Deal agencies were proud of such achievements, they were not above stretching the facts to make their point. Boulder Dam, for instance, was begun under President Hoover not FDR.

The other type of photograph typical to New Deal agencies was one that showed how Government programs were benefiting Americans. These might depict young, vigorous Civilian Conservation Corps (CCC) workers marching off to work in a national park (fig. 65). Or like the image of an all-black boxing team at a CCC camp in Danville, Illinois (fig. 69), they might stress how these programs improved the health or gave direction to CCC recruits. A photograph from the Works Progress Administration's Federal Theatre Project, which provided employment to actors, directors, and others in theatrical professions, shows Orson Welles in a performance of *Doctor Faustus*. This is another image that sends the message that New Deal programs did more than provide employment. They allowed for creativity and made valuable additions to American culture (fig. 78).

But whatever the achievements of the New Deal, it never managed to accomplish its most important goal—ending the Depression. And while many of the Depression-era photographs document progress, others testify that by the early 1940s, the Depression's grip was still strong. Irving Rusinow's photographs from Haskell County, Kansas, show that the social dislocation created by the droughts of the early thirties was still very much in evidence by April 1941 (fig. 76). Rondal Partridge's images of California (fig. 74), taken a year earlier, emphasized that unemployment remained high and that the practice of young people jumping freight trains in hope of a better life was still common. Finally, L.C. Harmon's photograph of two youngsters working in the beet fields of Nebraska points out that despite increasing Federal regulation, child labor continued in agricultural occupations (fig. 75).

A World in Flames

In size, geographic scope, and sheer destructiveness, World War II dwarfs all other conflicts in human history. When it was over, hundreds of cities lay in ruin, and 50 million people were dead. Millions of people were injured, displaced, or impoverished. Although the war had begun in September 1939, the United States did not enter the struggle until after the Japanese attack on Pearl Harbor, Hawaii, on December 7, 1941. For the next 3½ years, few elements of American society were left untouched by the war effort. On the fighting fronts, American soldiers, sailors, and airmen fought and often died in places many had never heard of a few years earlier. At home, mobilizing the country meant boosting industrial production, regulating the economy, and rationing consumer goods.

World War II also inspired millions of photographs. Photographers from agencies such as the Office of War Information recorded life on the homefront and mobilization of the economy. The Armed Forces also employed photographers in every theater of war. Improvements in camera technology and film permitted these men and women to get closer to combat than ever before. Other technologies—radiographs, cable, and the telephone—allowed images and stories to be sent from front lines in a matter of hours. While military censors often restricted what the American people saw, photographers still managed to eloquently capture much of the war's range, bravery, cruelty, and violence.

If the New Deal projects demonstrated how photography could be employed to support Government programs, then World War II saw even more far-reaching efforts to use photography as a tool to shape public opinion. U.S. policy makers believed that war in the modern world was more than battles between armies; whole societies were now at war with one another. The conflict would test not only a nation's armed forces but its industrial might, agricultural capacity, technological expertise, economic strength, and the resolve of its population.

The Government was quick to see the value of photography in such a struggle. The United States had been drifting toward war for years, but the shock and disbelief Americans felt in the wake of Pearl Harbor were still profound. Photographs were one way the Government could bring the war home to the American people, convince them of its seriousness, and motivate them to work harder and sacrifice more. A photograph, such as one of the U.S.S. *Shaw* exploding during the Pearl Harbor attack (fig. 91), could shake Americans out of their denial and get them to focus quickly on the grim tasks ahead. Photographs of ship construction or aircraft and tank manufacturing taught those at home the importance of industrial production to the war effort. Images of ethnic groups working together could teach the necessity of national unity in the midst of crisis.

It is easy to see the usefulness of photography for the war effort, but it is also understandable that the Government would want to control what Americans saw. During World War II, the Federal Government exercised extraordinary powers over the distribution of information. Military and industrial details thought to be useful to the enemy were censored, and the Government created a special bureau, the Office of War Information (OWI), to channel news in positive directions. This wartime news management extended to photography. Photographers, whether they were employed by the armed services, OWI, or the commercial press, were not usually restricted as to what subjects they could or could not shoot. Instead, they submitted their film to censors, who reviewed their images for violations.

Photographs were censored for a variety of reasons. Some wartime restrictions—photographs of top-secret sites or of troop movements that might aid the enemy—are easily understandable. The reasons why others were censored are not so obvious. Early in the war, for example, the public saw very few images of dead or badly wounded Americans. For more than a year after Pearl Harbor, military censors routinely restricted such photographs. By spring 1943, however, some OWI officials worried that a string of Allied victories early in the year would lead to overconfidence and complacency on the homefront. An OWI memorandum supporting the release of more casualty images argued that the photographs would shock Americans out of their "ostrich-like optimism" and bring home "the actual suffering of our fighters."

In September 1943 the military distributed the first of these graphic photographs. That same month *Life* magazine published one, a strikingly composed image by George Strock of three dead U.S. soldiers sprawled on a beach at Buna, New Guinea. In the months to come, until the end of the war, the American public would see an increasing number of photographs that showed American dead. However, the faces of the corpses were always turned away from the camera (fig. 95). Likewise, readers on the homefront seldom saw the ghastly effects of bullets or shrapnel on American bodies. Such images of enemy dead or wounded, however, were more commonplace.

Censorship was only one way the Government tried to control what the American people saw. The other approach, news management, was provided by the Office of War Information. OWI did not see itself as a censor. Instead, it saw its job as providing the American public with the information it needed to win the war. Director Elmer Davis was a respected journalist whose solution to balancing wartime restrictions with the ideals of a free press was a "strategy of truth." If the American people were presented with "the facts," they would understand what was at stake in the war and respond accordingly. This strategy left many unanswered questions about which "facts" the public needed to know and

Bureau of Special Services
3515 Soc Sec Bldg
Washington D C

OWI-IG-1

OPERATING POLICIES to be observed by Domestic Branch, Office of War Information

MAY 1943.

For your guidance ..

These are the major policies to guide operations of the Domestic Branch, Office of War Information:

1. We deal in one plain commodity—the facts the people of this country need to win the war. We must supply information about the fundamental war issues, about problems that demand attention and cooperation, about the things people must do to help themselves and their nation.

2. It is our assigned function to coordinate war information activities of all government departments and agencies. We are directed to prevent avoidable conflicts in information issued by individual agencies. In exercising our duties, we are concerned not merely with the negative function of preventing confusion, but with the positive function of seeing that the people get clear and correct information.

3. Within the limits of our resources, the facilities of the Domestic Branch are placed at the disposal of other government agencies in the planning of war-related informational activities within their sphere of responsibility.

4. We have no authority to make government policies, except such as concern the dissemination of war information. The material we issue must adhere to such policies as have been duly adopted by Congress and executive authority. Our defined functions therefore cannot permit us to take sides or to advocate or oppose social, political or economic reforms.

5. The Office of War Information is not charged with the maintenance of national morale. It is our conviction that once the people understand the facts about the war, and the reasons for measures taken in the prosecution of the war, national morale will be taken care of by the people themselves.

6. The Office of War Information will not, and does not want to, curtail the open-door policy that has always prevailed in the dealings of the Government with press and radio and other news media.

7. We have no concern with censorship—a function that has been entrusted to the Office of Censorship. We do not request public media to refrain from the presentation of any story or aspect of war information. It is, however, the obligation of OWI Domestic Branch personnel to become familiar with the press and radio codes of the Office of Censorship so as to be advised of the powers of that office. We may, at any time, provide public media with facts that will correct information believed untrue. At no time may we say or imply that any information *cannot* be printed or broadcast.

8. The responsibility for withholding information on the grounds that its release may endanger the national security rests with the armed forces and not with the Office of War Information. Our functions in this connection are two-fold: (a) to assist government agencies in securing rulings from the appropriate military and naval authorities; (b) to present to these authorities the point of view of the public so as

who would decide what these facts were, but it was nevertheless true that the American press was much freer in its coverage than its European counterparts were.

OWI homefront photography projects continued many of the approaches used by the FSA and other Depression agencies. In fact, Roy Stryker and many of his photographers simply transferred over to OWI when the FSA was shut down. OWI photographers like Edwin Rosskam, Russell Lee, Gordon Parks, Roger Smith, Esther Bubley, and Jack Delano continued to shoot many of the same kinds of documentary photographs as they had for the FSA. Their work still featured smalltown America and scenes of everyday life, American industry, and community. With the war, however, came some change in emphasis. Gone were the photos of impoverished farmers, the unemployed, and urban soup lines. Stryker fought to preserve as much of the tougher, FSA-style documentary approach as he could, but his instructions to OWI photographers still reflected the altered wartime context. He asked them to concentrate on images that would prove "useful" to the war effort. He also wrote to his pho-

tographers suggesting that they shoot photos showing "lots of food, strong husky Americans, machinery, show it as big and powerful, good highways, spaciousness. Also watch for such things as good schools, freedom of education, church services meetings of all kinds."

This sort of emphasis can also be seen in individual OWI photographs such as that by Edwin Rosskam of workers in a payline at the Baton Rouge Esso Refinery (fig. 102). The men are healthy, well fed and dressed, and presumably well payed. All are pictured as unique individuals, freely giving their labor. They represent a sharp contrast to the images of slave labor in Allied depictions of life in Axis-occupied nations. The workers also embody the notion that America brought almost limitless human resources to the Allied war effort. Another OWI photograph, this one by pioneering African American Government photographer Roger Smith, promotes national unity as a powerful weapon in the war against Germany and Japan (fig. 104). Like many other wartime photographs and propaganda posters, this image showed Americans of different ethnic backgrounds working and fighting together toward the common goal of defeating the Axis and its ideology of racial superiority.

Examining the weekly bulletins issued by OWI's Picture Division gives some sense of the kinds of battlefront photographs the agency believed would advance the Allied cause. During the summer of 1944, for example, the main theme OWI wanted to "hammer" was that of **"Axis Doom"** and the Allies' **"Overwhelming Force"** and **"Overwhelming Superiority."** A photograph taken by an Army Signal Corps photographer during the fighting near St. Lo, France, evokes just the sort of message OWI was looking for (fig. 92). A U.S. armored vehicle fires its gun at close range; shell casings litter the ground around it. A single American soldier stands nearby. Caption information only adds to the impression of invincibility. The armor "blasts Nazis fleeing St. Lo." Overall, the message is certainly one of "overwhelming force." All this firepower seems to place the soldier in less danger. Perhaps, we would like to believe, the artillery will finish the job and close-in fighting will not be necessary.

The Picture Division's approach can also be seen in its coverage of German civilians. By late 1944, as Germany came under Allied attack, OWI was looking for photographs that not only supported the idea of "surrender on all fronts" but that also gave evidence of "low morale, defeatism, and resignation." This theme continued as U.S. troops pushed further into Germany and German society began to disintegrate. Another Signal Corps photograph, taken in March 1945, also demonstrates this theme. It shows an old woman standing in the middle of the street surveying the ruins of her home. On either side of her are emotionally unmoved American soldiers, who march away with their backs to the camera. By her expression, the woman is in shock, a fact reinforced by the caption, which describes her as "in despair" as she "surveys the hopeless wreckage of her home" (fig. 99).

But even with censorship and news management, combat photographers managed to convey the experience and consequences of war through many outstanding photographs. Few images catch a dramatic moment better than Coast Guardsman Robert Sargent's view out of an invasion landing craft as troops, laden with heavy gear and under fire, wade ashore on D-day (fig. 93). An unknown U.S. Navy photographer was responsible for the photograph of a Marine, his face etched with the terror and tension of battle, during the invasion of Peleliu Island in the Pacific theater, (fig. 97). And one does not want to imagine what may have been happening to the crew of the B-17 shown in an uncredited OWI photograph, which caught the plane on film as it disintegrated in flight (fig. 100).

In another notable image, Navy Lt. Barrett Gallagher freezes a touching moment during a burial at sea for the men of the U.S.S. *Intrepid* (fig. 94). The ceremony is simple, shorn of patriotic trappings such as flags or dress uniforms. The crew slowly drops a long line of bodies, placed into plain bags, into the ocean. One body is already falling toward the water while the others are about to be pushed over the edge of the ship. The dead are anonymous to our eyes, but the crew treats their lost shipmates almost tenderly, and we wonder how well they knew those they are burying. Gallagher's point of view creates a line cutting across the photo that clearly separates the ship from the ocean below. The line sets apart two worlds: one is familiar, symbolized by the ship, its crew, and the burial ceremony. The other, unknown and frightening, is symbolized by the vastness of the unfathomable sea.

Among the most unforgettable of the many World War II photographs within NARA's holdings are those of the Holocaust. American troops played key roles in the liberation of many of the German death camps, and Army photographers were on hand to record the horrors they found. Many of these images show the Nazi's monstrous work in explicit detail. An example is a photograph of an inmate at Camp Gusen in Austria (fig. 106). The just-liberated prisoner, wrapped in a blanket, stares blankly back at the camera. In another, a soldier sifts through some of the thousands of wedding rings taken from those murdered by the Nazis at Buchenwald (fig. 105). While it is less graphic than many Holocaust images, its meaning is still shockingly clear. Symbols of love, unity, and wholeness, wedding rings have become a way of comprehending the tremendous number of people killed in the camps. Moreover, each ring represents not just one person killed by the Nazis but a relationship and a family broken and lost forever.

Postwar America

Many Americans feared that victory in World War II would be followed by a return of 1930s-like hard times. Instead, postwar America experienced a dramatic economic expansion, sustained prosperity, and a huge population increase. Never before in U.S. history had the Nation gone through such a boom. The United States led the world by almost any economic measure. It manufactured half the world's goods, possessed over 40 percent of the world's income, and had by far the highest standard of living. Moreover, the end of the war brought not only an economic boom but a "baby boom," as well. In 1946, 3.4 million babies were born, a 20-percent increase over 1945; this population explosion created a demographic bubble that continued to expand into the early 1960s. This remarkable growth was matched by a faith, shared by a broad consensus of Americans, that society was moving forward and the future would see the continued progress of "free enterprise" and democracy, at home and abroad.

Economists saw these statistics as only the most measurable features of a new kind of economy. Whereas pre-World War II capitalism had been subject to severe boom and bust cycles, which created great disparities in wealth and power, the postwar economy was stable, progressive, and democratic. It had not only created abundance but was eliminating rigid economic classes. In the United States the working class was quickly becoming a middle class. Moreover, this "people's capitalism," or "free enterprise system" as it was often called, was democratic in nature, it was flexible enough to be used by the Nation to solve the country's social problems. To achieve this end, the Government counted on the expertise of the American scientific and business communities. Further, it could embrace Government sponsored welfare measures such as Social Security as well as private welfare "fringe benefits" provided by American businesses. American capitalism "works quite brilliantly," declared economist John Kenneth Galbraith in 1952. "When firing on all eight cylinders," enthused another economist a few years later, "our economy is a mighty engine of social progress."

That this "mighty engine" was transforming American society is evident from the Government images of the time. During the first few years after the war, photographers continued to capture smalltown America similar to those taken by Farm Security Administration (FSA) photographers in the 1930s. In 1946 Russell Lee, who worked for the FSA, took a series of photographs of coal-mining communities around the country for a project supported by the Department of the Interior and the United Mine Workers Union. One of these images, taken in 1946, shows a busy Saturday afternoon street in Welch, West Virginia (fig. 115). Welch was more prosperous in 1946 than it had been during the Depression, and cars and fashions had changed, but otherwise Lee's photo has the look of an earlier era. In contrast, by 1951, State Department photographer, Oliver Pfeiffer was recording a much different street scene. His photograph of Chicago highlights the fast-paced anonymity of urban living and the massive skyscrapers that housed American corporations (fig. 113).

Photos from the postwar years emphasized other transformations, as well. Ed Latcham's aerial view of Levittown, Pennsylvania (fig. 118), for example, depicts one of three suburban housing developments named after the developer William Levitt. Designed to meet the postwar demand for single-family housing, "Levittowns" featured affordable, quickly built homes, nearby shopping and recreation, and school and other community spaces provided by the developer at cost. Critics charged that suburbs like Levittown were uniform, had few trees, and were racially segregated, but they proved very popular, especially among former GI's returning to civilian life. Levittowns and similar suburban developments seemed to match the aspirations of postwar couples who wanted to own their own home away from the city, tend a lawn, and concentrate on raising a family.

Photographers also pictured life as it would ideally be lived in the suburbs. The focus of suburban living was the nuclear family—father, mother, and children not only living under one roof but relying on each other to meet their needs. This close-knit family, along with modern conveniences and economic abundance, would bring apparent fulfillment through what historian Elaine Tyler May has called "an energized and expressive personal life." The connection between consumer products and family life can be seen in a photograph, provided to the State Department by Westinghouse Electric Company, of a mother and daughter posing in their gleaming new kitchen surrounded by conveniently arranged modern appliances (fig 117). Another scene, this one from the late 1950s, shows a suburban Washington, DC, family watching television together (fig. 119). They are attractive and well dressed, and their home is tastefully furnished. One daughter drinks Coca-Cola. The scene oozes domestic contentment.

Of course, not all Americans shared in the economic boom or lived in suburban tranquility. The self-assured optimism of the postwar blinded many to the country's problems. While most Americans earned more money and lived more comfortably by the late 1940s, millions still struggled in Depression-style poverty. Prosperity had especially skipped over Southern and Appalachian States such as West Virginia and Kentucky. Photographs made during Russell Lee's trip to coal-mining regions reveal the depth of this poverty. His portrait of Mrs. John Whitehead, "wife of miner" in the "kitchen" of her three-room house (fig. 116), reflects the same despair found in the migrant camps and soup lines of the 1930s. Whitehead's company-owned home had neither running water nor electricity. She and her children were dirty, ill nourished, and without prospects of improving their lives. She was not alone. In 1947 one-third of all American homes had no running water, two-fifths had no toilets, and three-fifths had no central heating.

Coverage of such societal failings was unusual. This was largely because of the Cold War. As competition between the United States and the Soviet Union began to dominate the postwar era and became increasingly viewed as an ideological struggle between freedom and communism, U.S. Government photography increasingly became an instrument of American foreign policy. This was not a wholly new development. Many of the Office of War Information's wartime publications and exhibits had also addressed foreign rather than domestic audiences, but by the early 1950s, some of the biggest Federal photography projects were being run out of the State Department for overseas consumption. The photographs from these projects emphasized American social and economic progress, downplayed problems or

3 **Topic**
Issue no. 51, 1969
*National Archives and Records Administration,
Records of the U.S. Information Agency*

Fashions From Africa
Educational Television
Young Politicians
View Their Parties

Topic
ISSUE NO. 51

shortcomings, and contrasted the vibrancy of American society with the drab totalitarianism of the Soviet Union and its allies.

It fell to the United States Information Agency (USIA) to serve as the Government's worldwide voice in the battle against communism. Created in 1953, the USIA (originally named the United States Information Service) still operates radio and television broadcasting networks, sponsors cultural exchanges, produces publications and exhibits, and runs libraries offering materials about the United States around the world. Its founders believed that in an age of mass communication, the Cold War would be fought not only through military and diplomatic means but through "public diplomacy"—directly communicating with foreign populations to influence public opinion.

Early USIA administrators realized photography could play a large role in this struggle. Many USIA publications were directed at mass audiences. They used photography to convey what the agency saw as the essence of American life—social and technological progress and cultural freedom—as well as to counter Soviet propaganda. Magazines such as *America Illustrated,* which was aimed at the Soviet Union and Eastern Europe, and *Topic,* which was aimed at sub-Saharan Africa (fig. 3), mimicked glossy American photomagazines such as *Life* and *Look.* Stories in these magazines varied from serious analyses of American politics, culture, and economics to lighter spreads on sports, fashion, and music. In their pursuit of illustrations, USIA staffers compiled huge files containing hundreds of thousands of negatives and prints. Photographs in these magazines were often gathered from sources outside the Government, a practice that made USIA publications appear like the commercial magazines after which they were modeled. Other USIA photo needs were met by USIA staff photographers. NARA's USIA photography holdings include its enormous "master file" of photographs, examples of USIA publications, photo "morgues" for some of its publications, and examples of staff and "stringer" assignments.

USIA "picture stories" were one device used to spread positive news about America and democracy. Created by the agency's International Press Service for distribution to State Department posts around the world, these heavily illustrated stories lauded the American economic and political systems. The 1957 picture story entitled "Lunchbox Capitalists"

4   **Proof sheet for the picture story** "Lunchbox Capitalists"
National Archives and Records Administration, Records of the U.S. Information Agency

✴ During his lunch hour, electrician Paul Craft reads a newspaper of the financial world, The Wall Street Journal, to see how his investments are progressing.   Craft works at the Monsanto Chemical Company

Columbia, Tennessee, which mines and refines chemical ores Along with approximately 40,000 other employees, he shares in the ownership of the company through the purchase of company stock

Lunchbox Capitalists

An increasing number of American workers are buying shares of stock in the companies they work for, thus becoming part owners and sharing in the profits. The firms are encouraging investment by offering stock to employees below its current sale price, thus acquiring new funds for research, expansion, and developing better tools and techniques which increase productivity.   The result is higher pay for a shorter work-week, giving employees more time to spend with their families and in social and civic pursuits

IPS Advance Proof

(fig. 4) described the spread of profit sharing and employee stock ownership plans in the United States. It sought to illustrate the progressive nature of American capitalism and how it had produced prosperous workers who enjoyed an enviable standard of living, plenty of leisure time for "social and civic pursuits," and the opportunity to become "part owners" who shared in the profits of giant corporations.

Other picture stories voiced similar themes. The author of "Tour for Khrushchev—The Real America" (ca. 1959), Democratic Presidential nominee Adlai Stevenson, chose sites that would "open the eyes" of Soviet leader Nakita Khrushchev during his upcoming trip to the United States. Stevenson suggested stopping at "a large industrial plant" to witness how modern capitalism works, observe healthful working conditions, and meet well-off workers. In the more militant "Comrades, You Lied to Me" (ca. 1959), a Hungarian expatriate photographed the America he believed demonstrated the Communist falsehoods he had accepted before moving to the United States. One photo showed a modern supermarket with a full-service bakery, where instead of waiting for hours as an Eastern European patron might, "without waiting for a minute you have a choice of many kinds of bread and bakery."

The Cold War struggle between communism and democracy also led to a terrifying and hugely expensive arms race between the Soviet Union and the United States. While the world mercifully managed to escape a nuclear exchange, the Cold War occasionally turned decidedly "hot." A bloody example was in Korea, a nation divided after World War II into the Soviet-and-Chinese-supported North and the American-backed South. When the North invaded the South on June 25, 1950, Soviet and Chinese leaders thought the fighting would end quickly and the United States would not intervene. Instead, President Harry Truman (fig. 114), acting under a United Nations' Security Council resolution and invoking his powers as Commander in Chief, deployed two U.S. divisions in Korea. For the next 3 years, vicious fighting raged up and down the Korean peninsula, leaving almost 34,000 Americans dead and almost 4 million casualties on all sides by the time an armistice was signed in July 1953.

The war was covered closely by military photographers. Some images, such as Pfc. C.T. Wehner's photo of U.S. Marines rounding up captured Chinese troops (fig. 120), were clearly propagandistic, designed to demonstrate American superiority and promote confidence and patriotism at home. Others were more honest in their depiction of the war. One was Sgt. Al Chang's touching photo (fig. 122), taken for the Army Signal Corps, of an American infantryman cradling his grief-wracked compatriot after the latter had learned his buddy had been killed. The photo showed how far Government coverage of combat had come since the early 1940s. Such a photo may have been taken by a military photographer during World War II, but it seems unlikely it would have been released, at least in the war's early years. In 1950 Chang's photograph was reproduced widely in the Nation's newspapers and magazines.

At one point the war was going so badly that President Truman briefly considered using nuclear weapons. By the early 1950s, the American and Soviet nuclear arsenals had grown dramatically. But much was still unknown about the effects of such weapons, especially about the danger of radiation they produced, and both sides engaged in routine testing of nuclear devices. Between 1946 and 1961, the United States conducted 203 tests at the Atomic Energy Commission's testsites in the South Pacific and Nevada. In 1951 at the Nevada testsite, military planners, eager to study the bomb's effects, conducted a series of tests while soldiers watched nearby (fig. 121). That same year, during a test called Operation Greenhouse near the South Pacific island of Enewetak, an Air Force photographer caught VIP observers illuminated by the flash of an atomic bomb, lounging like tourists in Adirondack chairs on the "patio" of the Officers' Beach Club (fig. 124), their eyes shielded by protective goggles.

Atomic testing, especially when international tensions ran high, increased the chances that weapons of mass destruction might be used. This possibility raised the question, how would Americans survive a nuclear attack? One answer provided by the Government was the building of fallout shelters. By 1961 about 1500 shelters had been built around the country, a number strongly influenced by elevated tensions that year. The Soviet Union and the United States clashed when the Soviets blocked access to the city of West Berlin. On July 25, President John F. Kennedy addressed the Nation and warned that force might be necessary to keep the city supplied. In addition, the President asked Congress to appropriate $93 million for fallout shelters. In September *Life* magazine ran an article entitled "How You Can Survive Fallout," which described home shelters, along with a Presidential letter suggesting that readers "consider seriously" the issues raised by *Life*.

What followed was "the fallout shelter craze of 1961." Over the next few months, more than 22 million copies of *Family Fallout Shelter*, the Office of Civil Defense's (OCD) guide to building and stocking shelters, were distributed, and thousands of Americans built and stocked these havens. Private companies sprang up to meet the demand. Some stressed the peacetime uses of shelters as well as their protective qualities. Shelter's added "a highly livable room" for only a small investment. They could serve as a darkroom, an extra bedroom, or as a den, where the "man of the house" could "check bank statements, read, and tend to his stamp collection without interruption."

In the early 1960s, OCD took a series of photos to publicize Louis Severance's shelter near Akron, Michigan. It had a small kitchen, a ventilation system, and a bathroom and cost about $1,000. It also had a 10-inch reinforced concrete ceiling and an escape hatch. A photograph of Severance's shelter (fig. 125) depicts it as a cozy hideaway. Father and son lie on their bunks reading. Familiar supermarket foods such as Campbell's and Lipton's soups, and Del Monte juices, line the shelves. A portable radio, plastic forks and spoons, and disposable plates add to the impression that 2 weeks inside the shelter would be more like sharing a family camping adventure than living through a nuclear nightmare. Severance, for his part, was quite pragmatic. He had wanted to build a shelter "ever

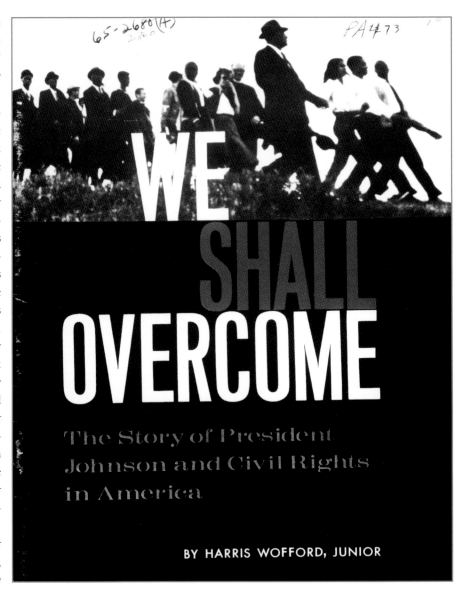

5 **We Shall Overcome: The Story of President Johnson and Civil Rights in America**
Story by Harris Wofford, Jr., 1965
National Archives and Records Administration, Records of the U.S. Information Agency

24

since I was convinced what damage H-bombs can do. . . Just as with my chicken farm, when there's a need I build it."

Although Cold War tensions frightened most Americans, many were otherwise enjoying the benefits of a booming economy. Most African Americans, however, were left out of the promise of the postwar years. While the economic circumstances of many black Americans had improved during World War II, millions, especially in the South, still suffered from racial segregation (fig. 127), poverty, and sometimes racial violence. By the late 1950s, however, there had been several notable and courageous challenges to segregation. A landmark 1954 Supreme Court ruling calling segregated schooling inherently unequal raised the hopes of black Americans. As a result of the ruling, nine black students, backed by Federal troops, integrated a Little Rock, Arkansas high school in 1957. Some months earlier, in December 1955, Rosa Parks, a Montgomery Alabama seamstress, refused to give up her bus seat to a white person and was subsequently arrested. Her arrest sparked a successful year-long bus boycott led by a young, charismatic Baptist minister, named Martin Luther King, Jr. (fig. 130).

By the early 1960s, these pathbreaking events had sparked a broadly based, increasingly assertive movement for black civil rights. In the face of enraged white resistance—including beatings, attacks by police dogs, bombings, and shootings—southern blacks and their northern supporters marched, boycotted, sat down, and mounted court challenges against segregation and racial inequality. It is estimated that in 1963 there were more than 20,000 people arrested in 930 civil rights demonstrations in 115 cities in 11 Southern States. By far the largest of these was the August 28 March on Washington, DC. This peaceful demonstration, which was attended by between 200,000 and 500,000 people and was the occasion for Martin Luther King's famous "I have a dream" speech, received extensive photographic coverage. Many of the resulting images were exuberant crowd and march scenes, but one USIA photographer chose a more intimate view of a young marcher (fig. 126).

The civil rights movement posed a dilemma for the USIA. Because of its role in supporting U.S. foreign policy, it sometimes glossed over problems in American society. By the 1960s, however, the civil rights movement had become so dramatic and newsworthy that USIA could hardly avoid covering it. The publication *We Shall Overcome* straightforwardly addressed the problems of discrimination that gave rise to the movement. The cover featured James Karales's dramatic photograph taken of the Selma to Montgomery, Alabama, voting rights march. But inside this pamphlet, President Lyndon Johnson is presented as the central protagonist for change. While there are a few photographs of blacks protesting, portraits of the President predominate. He is seen meeting with civil rights leaders, addressing Congress, signing legislation, and presenting an award to a young black woman. Often these images are paired with Johnson's words. The President is seen at the forefront of the struggle for civil rights, leading a Government that responds quickly to injustices and provides legislative solutions that demonstrate the flexibility and basic fairness of the American political system.

Century's End

Around 1965 the optimistic mood within American society that had persisted from the mid-1950s into the early 1960s began to shatter. The reasons for this fragmentation were twofold: the war in Vietnam and social unrest at home. American involvement in Vietnam began in the late 1950s, a product of a foreign policy that held that containing communism required committing American military and economic power to stop its spread. At first the United States provided economic and military aid and a few hundred military advisors to assist South Vietnam in its war with Communist North Vietnam. By the end of the Kennedy administration, however, there were almost 17,000 such "advisors" authorized to accompany South Vietnamese troops into combat. After Kennedy's assassination in 1963, President Johnson continued to send more men and aid to South Vietnam. After 1965 the number of American ground troops and casualties increased dramatically. By early 1968 there were more than 500,000 military personnel in Vietnam, and by the end of the year, the number of Americans dead, wounded, or missing had increased to 130,000.

Given this commitment of personnel, it is not surprising that a large number of the National Archives photographs from the mid-to-late 1960s through the early 1970s deal with the Vietnam War and that most of these tens of thousands of images are photographs produced by the Armed Forces. The military services used their photographic units, as they had previously, to record their activities in Vietnam, and their work captured a wide range of activities. They photographed equipment, dignitaries, entertainment for the troops, construction projects, educational and medical projects, and the Vietnamese countryside. Given the controversial nature of the war, it is also not surprising that these official photographers were often asked to counter negative press coverage of the war and were given official guidance to avoid showing American soldiers or U.S. policies in a bad light.

Vietnam photographers went into combat alongside the front-line soldier and suffered from the same conditions. "Every photograph you look at, there's a photographer right there," recalled one. "If you see pain in the photograph, a photographer recorded that pain in the heat, the humidity, the mud, the leeches and all the rest." This intimate view of the war, along with a determination to tell the story of the war from the footsoldiers point of view, won the confidence of the troops and often tempted combat photographers to ignore official guidelines and look for the best possible pictures. As one picture taker put it, "What the photographers did was worth doing—maybe not for the reasons the military said. They just felt what the soldiers were going through was worth saving."

Their efforts resulted in photographs that sensitively document the growing American involvement in Vietnam. In August 1965, shortly after President Johnson ordered one of the first major troop buildups, an unknown Marine Corps photographer witnessed the arrival of the 3d Marine Division in Da Nang, South Vietnam. This simple, straightforward portrait of a marine disembarking from an airplane not only captured one soldier's youth and innocence but could also symbolize America's innocence and idealism before it became deeply involved in the war (fig. 136).

A photograph from later in the war by Army Spc. Thomas Lykens shows a row of Huey helicopters near the Cambodian border in the remote Central Highlands of South Vietnam (fig. 138). Examining this image provides some idea of the depth of the American commitment to South Vietnam by 1969 as well as the technological might the United States had deployed there. Pvt. L. Paul Epley's somewhat surreal photograph of Long Kanh Provence, northeast of Saigon, in 1966 was a classic image depicting the costs of war. Two men of the 173d Airborne Brigade stand waiting for a helicopter to evacuate them from the scene of a firefight. According to the caption, one of the soldiers "lifts his battle weary eyes to the heavens, as if to ask why?" Nearby is the body of a fellow soldier covered with what would become a symbol of the war's futility—a bodybag (fig. 135).

After 1965, as more Americans fought and died in Southeast Asia, war protesters became more vocal, as did supporters of the U.S. Government's Vietnam policies. The liberal coalition that had passed historic civil rights legislation and the Great Society social programs began to splinter over issues such as the war, crime, poverty, and race. Early opponents of the war, most of them on the far left of the political spectrum, had constituted only a small minority. By late 1969, however, several opinion polls showed that the majority of Americans opposed the war and that this opposition was growing in middle America. As debate over Vietnam became more contentious, American society became increasingly polarized by the war itself, the harsh and uncompromising arguments put forth by both sides, and by related issues such as the patriotism of antiwar demonstrators and the fairness of the military draft.

Many college-age youth supported the war and even volunteered to fight in Vietnam, but it is nevertheless true that the antiwar movement gained much of its support from university students. Among many of these young people, opposition to the war was sometimes tied to a wider rejection of middle-class values and on the adoption of a "counter cultural" lifestyle, which included drug use, sexual freedom, "acid rock," and a new and defiant mode of fashion. While American society in the late 1960s did seem split roughly along generational lines, it is easy to exaggerate and stereotype such behavior. Signal Corps S. Sgt. Albert Simpson's photo of the 1967 antiwar demonstration at the Pentagon (fig. 139) reveals that there was also a split between young people. In the photo, demonstrators and military police, many of them the same age, face off. Soon after this photo was taken, the demonstration turned violent as the approximately 20,000 demonstrators, were driven from the Pentagon grounds.

The social unrest of the late sixties was not always tied to the Vietnam War. Starting in the summer of 1965 with the riots in Watts, a predominately black section of Los Angeles, America's poverty-wracked inner cities went through 4 years of sporadic rioting. The worst came in the summer of 1967 in Newark, New Jersey; Detroit, Michigan; Tampa, Florida; and Atlanta, Georgia. The Detroit riot lasted almost a week before National Guardsmen and police restored order, but by that time, thousands of buildings were burned or looted, hundreds were injured, and 43 people were dead. Afterward, volunteers from VISTA (Vol-

unteers In Service to America) came to assist in the riot torn city. A photographer recording their efforts took pictures of the destruction and the continued presence of the National Guard (fig. 140).

Another casualty of the war and social unrest was President Lyndon Johnson. During his slightly more than 5 years as President (1964–69), Johnson had many achievements he could point to with pride, including the 1964 Civil Rights Act, the 1965 Voting Rights Act, the creation of Head Start, (an education program for preschoolers), Medicaid (health insurance for the poor), and Medicare (health insurance for the elderly). These and other legislative victories completed much of the agenda liberals had worked for since the New Deal of the 1930s, but Johnson struggled to understand the widespread opposition to his Vietnam policies and the racial violence sweeping through American cities. His firm belief that a line had to be drawn in Vietnam put him under tremendous pressure as antiwar sentiment built.

In March 1968 Johnson announced that he would not run for reelection that fall. The pressure, however, continued to build with events such as the assassinations of Martin Luther King, Jr. and Robert Kennedy and the rioting that followed King's death. By the summer of 1968, when White House photographer Jack Knightlinger photographed Johnson listening to a tape recording from his son-in-law, Charles Robb, a Marine Corps company commander in Vietnam, the stress must have been enormous. While the anguish the President is experiencing in the photograph was specifically related to Robb's tape, Knightlinger's photograph seems to perfectly capture Johnson's political agony, as well (fig. 137).

Lyndon Johnson's Presidency ended in 1969. The new President, Richard M. Nixon, was an enigmatic, contradictory man who had been elected largely on his pledges to end the war in Vietnam "with honor" and get tough on crime. Although a longtime foe of Communism, as President, Nixon moved American foreign policy in new directions by conducting a rapprochement with the Soviet Union. He also began to normalize relations with Communist China, traveling there in 1972 (fig. 143). An opponent of big government, during his presidency Nixon saw the Federal workforce grow and even created new departments such as the Environmental Protection Agency. But Richard Nixon's presidency will always be tied to what has come to be known as the Watergate affair. Watergate was a web of scandals that began in 1972 with the arrest of seven employees of the Committee to Re-Elect the President who were

Crop dusting near Calipatria, California, 1972
Charles O'Rear—Photo No. 0026–121–15 S–74

Birmingham, Alabama, 1972
LeRoy Woodson—Photo No. 0008–053–28 S–52

Burning discarded auto batteries near Houston, Texas, 1972
Marc St. Gil—Photo No. 0018–001–16 S–42

Trouble on the Ohio River, 1972
Bill Strode—Photo No. 0004–026–35 S–36

Subway car, New York City, 1973
Erik Calonius—Photo No. 0070–002–36 S–24

Cattle drive in southwest Colorado, 1972
Bill Gillette—Photo No. 0032–032–22 S–15

A SAMPLE OF IMAGES in the *DOCUMERICA* image system and a selection from EPA's exhibition *Our Only World* touring the Nation under auspices of the Smithsonian Institution.

trying to break into the Democratic National Headquarters in the Watergate apartment complex in Washington, DC. A series of revelations in the press and televised congressional hearings, including the disclosure of related tape recordings from the Oval Office demonstrated that Nixon and his aides had attempted to cover up his administration's involvement. The revelations and subsequent public outrage eventually led to Nixon's resignation and to his dramatic departure from the White House on August 9, 1974 (fig. 147).

It was left to Richard Nixon's successor, Gerald R. Ford (fig. 150), to preside over the sad conclusion of America's involvement in Vietnam. Nixon had managed to extricate

6 **Sampler of the DOCUMERICA images used in the Smithsonian Institution exhibition "Our Only World"**
ca. 1973
National Archives and Records Administration, Records of the Environmental Protection Agency

American troops from Vietnam through a combination of tough diplomacy, bombing raids on North Vietnam, "Vietnamization" (increasing military aid to South Vietnamese forces so they could defend themselves rather than relying on the U.S.), and measured American troop withdrawals. He also won the release of American prisoners of war held in the North (fig. 144). After Nixon's resignation, Ford wanted to continue sending support to South Vietnam, but Congress prevented it. By April 1975 the South Vietnamese Government, stripped of U.S. aid, collapsed under an onslaught of Viet Cong and North Vietnamese attacks. As the Communists advanced, refugees left South Vietnam in small boats. Navy photographer Mike McGougan was onboard the U.S.S. *Durham* as the ship picked up 3,000 such refugees after the abandonment of the giant airbase at Cam Ranh Bay. McGougan's photograph (fig. 145) catches the desperation of the refugees as well as the lifesaving heroics of the American naval personnel.

Aside from Vietnam, one of the most-photographed Government activities in the latter part of the century was the U.S. space program. Beginning with the first satellite launches in the late 1950s, through the Moon missions of the early 1970s, and through the space shuttle missions of the 1980s, the National Aeronautics and Space Administration (NASA) documented space flight in minute detail. This scrutiny reflected not only the pathbreaking nature of NASA's work and its prodigious publicity efforts but also the enormous public interest in space flight.

The *Apollo* project, which put a man on the Moon, was particularly well covered. During the *Apollo 8* mission in December 1968, humans orbited the Moon for the first time. It was also the occasion for a remarkable photograph, taken by astronaut William Anders, of an "Earthrise" above the Moon (fig. 142). While this was not the first image of Earth from space, it is certainly the most famous. It reinforces the idea that the Earth is only a very small part of our solar system and simultaneously wipes out national boundaries and gives a new appreciation for the fragility of "the blue planet." Other justly famous photographs from the manned space program include Neil Armstrong's image of fellow astronaut Edwin E. "Buzz" Aldren's boot and bootprint on the lunar surface (fig. 141) and a 1983 photo of the ill-fated space shuttle *Challenger* as it appears to float above the Earth with its cargo door open (fig. 156).

The 1970s also saw one short-lived effort to create another large Government photography project. In 1972 the Environmental Protection Agency (EPA) began DOCUMERICA with the intention of "photographically documenting subjects of environmental concern in America." Over the next 4 years, EPA hired some of the Nation's most talented photographers, who traveled around the country recording a variety of subjects, usually in color. Many DOCUMERICA photos are of America's environmental problems, such as air and water pollution, highway clutter, and blighted housing, but photographers were given great leeway in the subjects they chose. This freedom resulted in a rich documentary picture of American society, not unlike the documentary projects of the 1930s upon which EPA's program was modeled. DOCUMERICA photographers recorded life on Indian reservations, in small Midwestern towns, and in America's inner cities. Subjects were as diverse as fly fishing, stockcar racing, cattle drives, fast-food restaurants, baseball, and concerts.

EPA hoped that DOCUMERICA would create a "visual baseline" of 1970s America from which future progress on environmental issues could be measured. More broadly, the project would tally the social and economic costs of environmental change and depict the Nation's successes and failures. One practical project was to have DOCUMERICA record air pollution as it existed in 1972. Later photographs would chart improvements and community compliance. In addition to these utilitarian benefits, EPA asked its photographers to document the environmental movement and depict Americans "doing their environmental thing." They were not to concentrate solely on "deplorable conditions" but to also "show the beauty of what is worth saving." In fact, it seemed almost anything was a potential DOCUMERICA subject. Gifford Hampshire, who headed the project, was fond of quoting environmentalist Barry Commoner's First Law of Ecology as DOCUMERICA's credo: "Everything is connected to everything else."

Despite this broad charge, many DOCUMERICA photographers were hired or chose to picture environmental problems. In one typical image, Leroy Woodson brought together the poor housing, poverty, and environmental difficulties that faced residents living in the shadow of a U.S. Steel plant in Birmingham, Alabama (fig. 146). 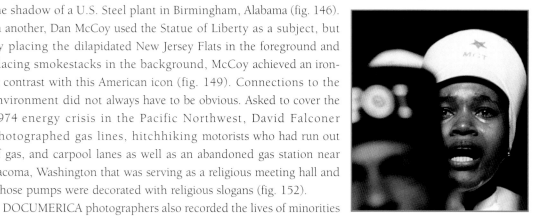 In another, Dan McCoy used the Statue of Liberty as a subject, but by placing the dilapidated New Jersey Flats in the foreground and placing smokestacks in the background, McCoy achieved an ironic contrast with this American icon (fig. 149). Connections to the environment did not always have to be obvious. Asked to cover the 1974 energy crisis in the Pacific Northwest, David Falconer photographed gas lines, hitchhiking motorists who had run out of gas, and carpool lanes as well as an abandoned gas station near Tacoma, Washington that was serving as a religious meeting hall and whose pumps were decorated with religious slogans (fig. 152).

DOCUMERICA photographers also recorded the lives of minorities and other ethnic groups. Terry and Lynthia Eiler traveled to the Four Corners area in Utah to photograph Hispanic migrant workers. One photo of these men and women, reminiscent of Dorothea Lange's Depression images, shows workers seeking shelter from a duststorm (fig. 148). In 1973 and again briefly in 1974, the future Pulitzer Prize-winning photographer John H. White worked for DOCUMERICA photographing Chicago, Illinois, especially its African American community. White saw his assignment as "an opportunity to capture a slice of life" and to draw attention to the "strengths, sorrows, and joys" within the city. One striking portrait of a member of the Black Muslims at a prayer meeting (fig.155) is typical of the work produced for this assignment, which also included photographs from the Chicago streets, housing projects, playgrounds, churches, and businesses.

For all its creativity, DOCUMERICA lasted for only a few years before Congress began to question the need for the project. EPA staff hoped that as they amassed more photographs, the press would generate positive publicity for the project and use DOCUMERICA images. EPA also tried to increase DOCUMERICA's visibility by sponsoring exhibits of project photographs. "Our Only World," was one such exhibit, created by the Smithsonian Institution's Traveling Exhibit Service. DOCUMERICA later took the photographs in this exhibit and made them available for purchase. EPA also distributed "samplers" showing a few of the DOCUMERICA images the public could purchase using its "image system," an early computerized database of DOCUMERICA photographs. Despite these efforts, DOCUMERICA failed to capture the attention of the public or the opinion makers who might have supported its continuation. Budget cuts ended the project in 1977.

By the late 1970s and early 1980s, the country, exhausted from years of turmoil, experienced a conservative revival that shaped not only the politics of both political parties but also public policy. The man most associated with this late 20th-century conservatism was

Ronald Reagan. During his two terms as President, Reagan presided over the most successful conservative coalition in 20th-century U.S. history. His proposed Federal income tax cuts, tough anticommunism, massive defense buildup, and efforts to shrink Johnson's Great Society social programs won the enthusiastic support of traditional Republicans, evangelical Protestants, and blue-collar Democrats. His ability to convey optimism about America's future while outlining a broad political agenda was unsurpassed. These skills, along with an affable personality that endeared him to millions, left him virtually untouched by critics. White House photographer Michael Evans's photograph (fig. 154) of the President speaking at a rally for Minnesota Senator David Durenberger, captures much of the President's determination and patriotism.

As the 20th century comes to a close we can only speculate as to the future of Federal photography and how changes in the way the Government approaches photographs will affect the holdings of the National Archives. On the one hand, improvements in camera technology and film have made it possible to have almost minute-by-minute coverage of important events and personalities. Such improvements have raised the numbers of photographs taken by Government photographers to unprecedented levels, and images arriving or scheduled to arrive at the National Archives and Records Administration will grow accordingly.

Surveys of Federal agencies by NARA archivists show that mountains of 20th-century photography sit in a variety formats at numerous Federal agencies. For example, the Secretary of Transportation's Photography Section holds more than 150,000 color and black and white negatives, prints, and other formats documenting the Department of Transportation's activities from the late 1940s to the 1990s. The Defense Visual Information Center has over 210,000 historic images of Armed Forces activities around the world from the 1980s and 1990s alone. The U.S. Geological Survey's Denver Photographic Laboratory maintains an image file of 250,000 prints with corresponding negatives and some 50,000 additional slides. Most impressive of all is NASA's Space Shuttle Project Engineering Office at the Kennedy Space Center in Florida which has generated an incredible 2.5 million color negatives! Other agency photo files are smaller, but often still number in the tens of thousands. And while not all of these images have been deemed permanently valuable, many will eventually become part of the National Archives.

On the other hand, over the last 20 years, as Federal agencies have experienced budget cutbacks, downsizing, and various forms of reorganization and "reinvention," they have reduced the size and scope of their photography operations. These reductions have meant not just smaller staffs and fewer resources but an end to most open-ended documentary photography projects, as well. Today, many Federal photographers often struggle to simply cover largely ceremonial events in Washington, DC, and are forced to forego many regional or field activities. In addition, some agencies have been abolished altogether, which often results in a sudden and somewhat disorganized influx of photographs to NARA.

Another casualty of smaller staffs and fewer resources has been the agency central photo file. Today, agency "master files" often consist of 35mm negative strips, contact sheets, or 3- by 5- or 4- by 5-inch "quick" prints processed by the same sort of commercial photo-labs used by the public, with only general assignment descriptions to serve as a guide to their subject. In contrast to the edited, indexed, and captioned central files of earlier years, many contemporary agency photo files were created for short-term publicity purposes rather than with an eye toward the historical record. Moreover, competing technologies such as television, video, and the Internet may encourage the Government and the public to rely less on still photography for visual information.

As a result of these changes, NARA still photography archivists will face stiff challenges in the years ahead to keep up with the volume and changing nature of the records accessioned into the National Archives as well as making them readily available. The number of agency photographs offered to NARA will increase sharply, but they will arrive in formats that are more difficult to work with and accompanied by fewer guides to their organization and by less complete descriptive information. Archivists will need to weed out non-permanent routine images to arrange new accessions and eventually prepare the detailed guides and finding aids that are useful to researchers. New technologies offer hope of quickening access to photographs. NARA, for example, has developed a pilot database on the World Wide Web, the NARA Information Locator (NAIL), that contains almost 374,000 descriptions and up to 120,000 digital copies of documents, including thousands of photographs. NAIL will serve as a prototype for an even more comprehensive online catalog.

Digital technology is a two-sided sword, however. Some Federal agencies, especially the Department of Defense, are already using digital cameras to record their activities. When such imagery eventually makes its way to NARA, it will raise many interesting archival issues about properly preserving these electronic files, assuring that correct captioning accompanies items, and making these digital images available to researchers in easy-to-use formats. Digital images also challenge our notion of "original" and "copy" and raise the possibility of images being altered.

This is not to say that contemporary Government photographers do not produce outstanding photographs. One example is the work of Gerald Dean, a photographer with the Department of Housing and Urban Development. Buried among the many strips of color negatives of largely ceremonial Department functions is his 1985 photo of Vice President George Bush at the opening of the Martin Luther King, Jr. Holiday Commission (fig. 153). Dean's marvelously ambiguous photo shows the Vice President, head in hand, seated in front of a portrait of Reverend King. Other exceptional late-20th-century images come from the Clinton administration; White House Photo Office photographers such as Barbara Kinney and Bob McNeeley have been able to move beyond traditional ceremonial, or "grip and grin," photographs to capture the mood and demeanor of the President, First Lady, and other well-known personalities (figs. 157–158).

A few things seem certain. Federal agencies will continue to document their actions photographically, and NARA will continue to be the most important repository for their historic images. Future generations will search the National Archives to find telling and important pictures from our time that are as historic to them as photographs from the earlier 20th century are to us. Images of the fall of the Berlin Wall, the Persian Gulf War, and the *Challenger* space shuttle explosion will take their places alongside those of the first flight of the Wright brothers, the D-day invasion, and the Moon landings. Just as important—since NARA's photography holdings are for the most part public records—is the fact that the National Archives will remain one of the few places that provides a wide overview of American and much of world history that is open and accessible. Its photographs will remain a unique and valuable resource, an invitation to browse, study, and consider not only the meaning of the contradictory 20th century but of future centuries as well. ∎

7 *See page viii:* "**Second Lieut. Paul Weir Cloud, still operator, photographic unit with 89th Division Newar Kyllburg, Germany**"
By an unknown photographer, January 16, 1919
National Archives and Records Administration, Records of the Office of the Chief Signal Officer (111-SC-51107)

8 *Opposite:* "**Sgt. Carl Weinke and Pfc. Ernest Marjoram, Signal Corps cameramen, wading through stream while following infantry troops in forward area during invasion at a beach in New Guinea. Red Beach 2, Tanahmerah**"
By T4c. Ernani D'Emidio, April 22, 1944
National Archives and Records Administration, Records of the Office of the Chief Signal Officer (111-SC-189623)

9 "Photograph of the Alaskan Yukon Pacific (A.Y.P.)
Exposition, entrance arches"
By an unknown photographer, Seattle, Washington, August 1909
National Archives and Records Administration,
Records of the Bureau of Public Roads
(30-N-2534)

10 "Avenue of Statues near Ming Tombs,
near Pekin (sic). Troop L, 6th Cavalry"
By Capt. C.F. O'Keefe, near Beijing, China,
1900
*National Archives and Records Administration,
Records of the Office of the Chief Signal Officer*
(111-SC-75112)

11 "Fifth Avenue in New York City on
Easter Sunday in 1900"
By an unknown photographer, 1900
*National Archives and Records Administration,
Records of the Bureau of Public Roads*
(30-N-18827)

12 "Hester Street, New York City"
By an unknown photographer, ca. 1903
National Archives and Records Administration,
Records of the Public Housing Administration
(196-GS-369)

13 "Steadman Ave. Nome, Alaska"
By an unknown photographer, July 1900
National Archives and Records Administration,
Records of the Office of the Chief Signal Officer
(111-SC-83797)

14 "The first ranger force in Yosemite. Left to right: Oliver Preen, Chief Ranger; Charles Bull, First Asst.; Jack Gayor, Second Asst.; Wayne Westfall; George McNab; Charles Leidig; Charles Adair; Archie Leonard; and Forest Townsley. Forest Townsley (now Chief Ranger) and Charles Adair are still on the Yosemite ranger force."
By Fiske, Yosemite National Park, California, 1915
National Archives and Records Administration–Pacific Region (San Francisco), Records of the National Park Service

15 "**Bandstand and rostrum erected soon after the landing of the Metlakahlans on Annette Island, Alaska**"
By an unknown photographer, Metlakahla, Annette Island, Alaska, ca. 1900
National Archives and Records Administration–Pacific Alaska Region (Anchorage), Henry S. Wellcome Collection (#648)

16 "Original Wright Brothers 1903 Aeroplane
('Kitty Hawk') in first flight, December 17,
1903, at Kitty Hawk, NC. Orville Wright at
controls. Wilbur Wright at right (First flight
was 12 seconds)."
By Orville Wright and John T. Daniels,
December 17, 1903
*National Archives and Records Administration, Records
of the War Department General and Special Staffs*
(165-WW-713-6)

17 "1913—Trying out the new assembly line"
By an unknown photographer, Detroit, Michigan, 1913
National Archives and Records Administration, Records of the Bureau of Public Roads
(30-N-49-1482)

18 "At Renault's Champagne Vaults, Egg Harbor, NJ"
By an unknown photographer, summer 1906
National Archives and Records Administration, Records of the Bureau of Plant Industry, Soils, and Agricultural Engineering
(54-HPN-8712)

19 "Municipal Lodging House. Shower bath."
By an unknown photographer, New York, New York, ca. 1903
National Archives and Records Administration, Records of the Public Housing Administration
(196-GS-1-670)

20 *Top:* "**Immigrant Children, Ellis
Island, New York**"
By Brown Brothers, ca. 1908
*National Archives and Records Administration,
Records of the Public Health Service*
(90-G-125-29)

21 *Bottom:* "**Immigrants Landing at Ellis
Island**"
By Brown Brothers, New York, New York,
ca. 1900
*National Archives and Records Administration,
Records of the Public Health Service*
(90-G-22D-42)

22 **"Lee Wai She and children"**
By an unknown photographer, Honolulu, Hawaii, 1913
National Archives and Records Administration–Pacific
Region (San Francisco), Records of the Immigration and
Naturalization Service
(case file #2989-c)

23 "The Sam McCall family of Wilcox County, Alabama"
By M.A. Crosby, 1910
National Archives and Records Administration, Records of the Bureau of Agricultural Economics (83-FA-5005)

24 "Condiment Stand in Center Market"
By an unknown photographer, Washington, DC, February 18, 1915
National Archives and Records Administration, Records of the Bureau of Agricultural Economics (83-G-3653)

25 "Party 'nature sliding' on the perpetual snow slopes below Paradise Glacier"
These parties are under guide direction. Individuals are equipped with the famous 'tin trousers.' "The seats of these trousers are paraffined. Parties are seated together on the snow and slide long distances."
By Jacobs, Mount Rainier National Park, Washington, ca. 1917
National Archives and Records Administration, Records of the National Park Service
(79-G-12A-2)

26 **"Agnes J. Quirk, Laboratory of Plant Pathology, U.S. Department of Agriculture, Washington, DC"**
By the Clinedinst Studio, October 26, 1916
National Archives and Records Administration, Records of the Office of the Secretary of Agriculture
(16-ES-247)

27 "View of the destruction brought about by the San Francisco Earthquake, 1906"
By H.W. Chadwick, April 1906
National Archives and Records Administration, Records of the Office of the Chief Signal Officer
(111-AGF-1A-1D)

28 *Bottom:* "Flood at Seward, Alaska, Sept. 10, 1917"
By an unknown photographer
National Archives and Records Administration, Records of the Office of Territories
(126-AR-13B-7)

29 "Funeral of Ludlow victims leaving Catholic Church"
By Dold, Trinidad, Colorado, 1914
National Archives and Records Administration,
General Records of the Department of Labor

d at Seward, Alaska, Sept. 10, 1917.

WALTER LUBKEN

From 1903 to 1917, Walter J. Lubken (1881–1960) was an official photographer for the U.S. Reclamation Service (USRS). During these years, Lubken took thousands of photographs documenting the Reclamation Service's irrigation projects across the American West. He recorded the progress of construction projects as well as USRS machinery and personnel. The agency also asked Lubken to photograph nearby towns and farms for a series of articles designed to promote settlement on land reclaimed from the desert through irrigation. Traveling with his large camera and glass-plate negatives, he documented 25 projects in 17 Western States. After leaving the Reclamation Service in 1917, Lubken also left professional photography until the 1930s, when he photographed the building of Boulder Dam.

Lubken's photographs capture both engineering feats and everyday life in the early-20th-century West. His optimistic images impress the viewer with the technological and

30 *Opposite:* "**Testing the subsurface—Drilling with diamond drills**"
By Walter J. Lubken for the Boise Irrigation Project, Idaho and Oregon, August 1910
National Archives and Records Administration, Records of the Bureau of Reclamation
(115-JC-384)

31 "**Gunnison tunnel opening; the arch at Montrose**"
By Walter J. Lubken for the Uncompahgre Irrigation Project, Colorado, September 23, 1909
National Archives and Records Administration, Records of the Bureau of Reclamation
(115-JAF-604)

social advances made by westerners. They make the point that progress and community had come to isolated, formerly barren places and that abundant opportunities awaited those willing to move west and work hard on the reclaimed land.

The National Archives holds both Lubken's photographic prints and many of his original glass-plate negatives among the records of the Bureau of Reclamation. There are also scattered Lubken photographs among the records of the Bureau of Indian Affairs and the U.S. Forest Service. ∎

32 "Dedication ceremonies of Roosevelt Dam, Col. Roosevelt speaking"
By Walter J. Lubken, Arizona, March 18, 1911
National Archives and Records Administration, Records of the Bureau of Reclamation
(115-JAA-2267)

33 "Interurban cars running through Main Street of Caldwell"
By Walter J. Lubken, Boise Irrigation Project, Caldwell, Idaho, February 21, 1910
National Archives and Records Administration, Records of the Bureau of Reclamation
(115-JC-305)

34 "U[nited] S[tates] R[eclamation] S[ervice] kitchen, mess hall, Avalon Dam"
By Walter J. Lubken, Carlsbad Irrigation Project, New Mexico, October 29, 1906
National Archives and Records Administration, Records of the Bureau of Reclamation
(115-JD-119)

Lewis Hine

For Lewis Wicks Hine (1874–1940) the camera was both a research tool and an instrument of social reform. Born in Oshkosh, Wisconsin, Hine studied sociology at the University of Chicago and Columbia and New York Universities. He began his career in 1904 photographing immigrants arriving in the United States at Ellis Island in New York Harbor. In 1908 he became photographer for the National Child Labor Committee (NCLC). Over the next decade, Hine documented child labor in American industry to aid the NCLC's lobbying efforts to end the practice. Between 1906 and 1908, he was a free-lance photographer for *The Survey*, a leading social reform magazine. In 1908, Hine photographed life in the steelmaking section of Pittsburgh, Pennsylvania for the influential study "The Pittsburgh Survey." During and after World War I, he documented American Red Cross relief work in Europe. In the 1920s and early 1930s, Hine made a series of "work portraits," which emphasized the human contribution to modern industry, and included photographs of the workers constructing New York City's Empire State Building. During the Great Depression, he again worked for the Red Cross, photographing drought relief in the American South, and for the Tennessee Valley Authority (TVA), documenting life in the mountains of eastern Tennessee. He also served as chief photographer for the

Works Progress Administration's (WPA) National Research Project, which studied changes in industry and their effect on employment.

The National Archives holds almost 2,000 Hine photographs, including examples of his child labor and Red Cross photographs, his work portraits, and his WPA and TVA images. ∎

35 *Opposite:* "**Some of the doffers and the Supt. Ten small boys and girls about this size out of a force of 40 employees. Catawba Cotton Mill. Newton, NC.**"
By Lewis Hine, December 21, 1908
National Archives and Records Administration, Records of the Children's Bureau
(102-LH-440)

36 "**Power house mechanic working on steam pump**"
By Lewis Hine, 1920
National Archives and Records Administration, Records of the Work Projects Administration
(69-RH-4L-2)

37 "Mt. Holyoke, Massachusetts—Paragon Rubber Co. and American Character Doll. Setting eyes in sleeping dolls (Jewish) A Plus."
By Lewis Hine, December 1936–February or July 1937
National Archives and Records Administration, Records of the Work Projects Administration (69-RP-60)

38 "In the Mill"
By Lewis Hine, Pittsburgh, Pennsylvania, 1909
National Archives and Records Administration, Records of the Work Projects Administration (69-RH-1K-3)

39 "Old-timer—keeping up with the
boys. Many structural workers are above
middle-age. Empire State [Building]."
By Lewis Hine, New York, New York, 1930
National Archives and Records Administration,
Records of the Work Projects Administration
(69-RH-4K-1)

40 "Liberty Loan Choir sings on the steps of City Hall, New York City, during third
Liberty Loan campaign. Bishop William Wilkinson leads the choir."
By Paul Thompson, April 1918
National Archives and Records Administration, Records of the Office of the Chief Signal Officer
(111-SC-16561)

41 "Sweethearts and relatives bidding fighting 69th Inf. N.Y. a fond goodbye."
By the Western Newspaper Union, August 1917
National Archives and Records Administration, Records of the War Department General and Special Staffs
(165-WW-476-1)

42 "American base hospital, France"
By an unknown photographer, ca. 1917–18
National Archives and Records Administration, Records of the Office of the Chief Signal Officer
(111-SC-4067)

43 "Liberty Day celebration, Camp Grant, Rockford, Illinois"
By Duce and McClymonds, ca. 1917–18
National Archives and Records Administration, Records of the War Department General and Special Staffs
(165-PP-37-12)

44 "Shipbuilders at the Grant-Smith-Porter Company's Gray's Harbor Yards"
By an unknown photographer, Aberdeen, Washington, 1917
National Archives and Records Administration, Records of the U.S. Shipping Board
(32-PW-5)

45 "Soldiers being mustered out at Camp Dix, New Jersey"
By Underwood and Underwood, 1918
National Archives and Records Administration, Records of the War Department General and Special Staffs
(165-WW-139-C-3)

46 "Some of the colored men of the 369th (15th N.Y.) Who won the Croix de Guerre for gallantry in action." Left to right. Front row: Pvt. Ed. Williams, Herbert Taylor, Pvt. Leon Fraitor, Pvt. Ralph Hawkins. Back row: Sgt. H. D. Prinas, Sgt. Dan Storms, Pvt. Joe Williams, Pvt. Alfred Hanley, and Cpl. T.W. Taylor."
By an unknown photographer, 1919
National Archives and Records Administration, Records of the War Department General and Special Staffs
(165-WW-127-8)

47 "Women Rivet Heaters and Passers on"
By an unknown photographer, Puget Sound
Navy Yard, Washington, May 29, 1919
National Archives and Records Administration,
Records of the Women's Bureau
(86-G-11F-7)

48 Potatoes become the "newest fighting
corps" in Iowa. A display in a drugstore store
window urges Iowans to eat more potatoes to
aid the war effort by conserving other foods.
By an unknown photographer, Maquoketa,
Iowa, July 1918
National Archives and Records Administration–
Central Plains Region, Records of the U.S. Food
Administration
(4.IA.1)

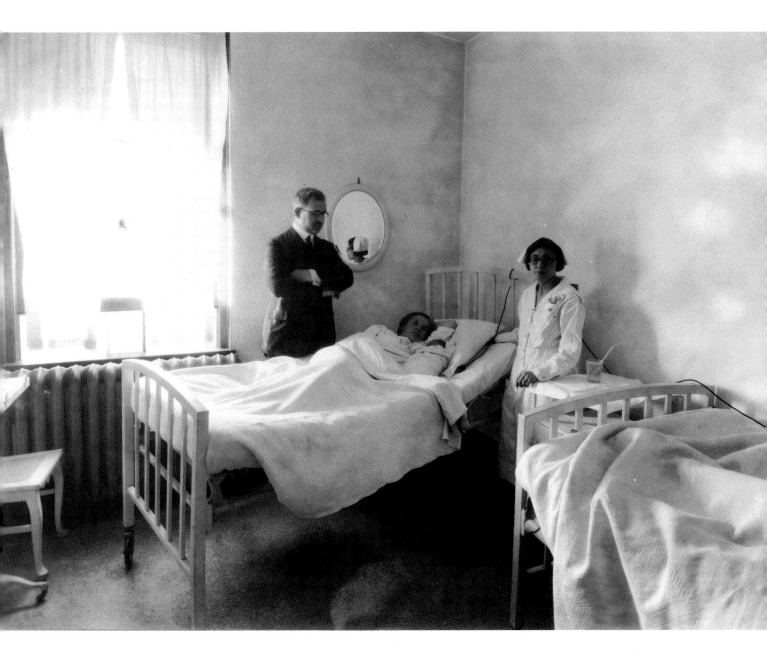

49 **"Community Hospital; Maternity Case"**
By an unknown photographer, Hutchison,
Minnesota, October 1924
National Archives and Records Administration,
Records of the Bureau of Agricultural Economics
(83-ML-10309)

50 "Girl Ushers for Chicago baseball games. Beatrice Solomon and Violet Flatow, the first baseball girl ushers, watching a game."
By Underwood and Underwood, Chicago, Illinois, July 1918
National Archives and Records Administration, Records of the War Department General and Special Staffs
(165-WW-595F-1)

KAISER WILSON

HAVE YOU FORGOTTEN YOUR SYMPATHY WITH THE POOR GERMANS BECAUSE THEY WERE NOT SELF-GOVERNED?

20,000,000 AMERICAN WOMEN ARE NOT SELF-GOVERNED.

TAKE THE BEAM OUT OF YOUR OWN EYE.

51 "Suffragette banner. One of the banners the women who picketed the White House carried."
By an unknown photographer, Washington, DC, 1918
National Archives and Records Administration, Records of the War Department General and Special Staffs
(165-WW-600A-5)

52 "Mysterious fliers who thrilled a gathering of the K[u] K[lux] K[lan] at a reception of officers of [the] Klan"
By an unknown photographer, Dayton, Ohio, 1924
National Archives and Records Administration, Records of the U.S. Information Agency
(306-NT-650-11)

53 *Opposite:* **"Trainees in Power Plant Operation at the State A.& E. College, West Raleigh, N.C."**
By an unknown photographer, 1921
National Archives and Records Administration, Records of the Veterans Administration
(15-VR-2H6)

54 **"Pilot Wm. C. Hopson, U.S. Mail Service Winter Flying Clothing."**
By an unknown photographer, Omaha, Nebraska, ca. 1926
National Archives and Records Administration, Records of the U.S. Postal Service
(28-MS-6E-1)

PILOT W. C. HOPSON
U.S MAIL SERVICE
WINTER FLYING CLOTHING

55 Royal Theater, Kansas City, Missouri.
The marquee advertises the movie *It*,
starring Clara Bow.
By the Commercial Photo Company,
Kansas City, Missouri, March 5, 1927
National Archives and Records
Administration–Central Plains Region, Records
of the District Courts of the United States
(21.WMO.KC.897)

56 President Herbert Hoover, Henry
Ford, Thomas Edison, and Harvey
Firestone at Edison's 82d birthday
celebration
By an unknown photographer, Fort Myers,
Florida, February 11, 1929
Herbert Hoover Library, National Archives
and Records Administration
(1929-12)

57 **Kong Wo Sang Co, Newcastle, California**
By an unknown photographer, 1926
National Archives and Records Administration–Pacific Region (San Francisco), Records of the Immigration and Naturalization Service
(case file #25103/7-20)

58 **"Brooklyn Center Village Store where Hennepin Co., Minn. Library has a deposit station."**
By an unknown photographer, ca. 1925
National Archives and Records Administration, Records of the Bureau of Agricultural Economics
(83-ML-15035)

59 **"Farmer reading his farm paper"**
By George W. Ackerman, Coryell County, Texas,
September 1931
National Archives and Records Administration,
Records of the Extension Service
(33-SC-15754c)

GEORGE ACKERMAN

During a nearly 40-year career with the Department of Agriculture, George W. Ackerman (1884–1962) estimated that he took over 50,000 photographs. Ackerman began working as a photographer for the Bureau of Plant Industry in 1910 at a salary of $900 a year. In 1917 he moved to the Federal Extension Service, and in that position, he traveled around the country photographing rural life. His photographs appeared in many private and Government agricultural publications, although they were not usually credited to him.

Today, many of Ackerman's photographs fill us with nostalgia for a simpler time, but this was not the photographer's intention. Instead, Ackerman was striving to show the improvements and progress that had come to the American farm in the 20th century. The rural life seen in his photographs is comfortable. Farmers are contented and prosperous people who face the future with confidence. They use the latest laborsaving devices and techniques. They and their neatly dressed wives and children enjoy modern conveniences and social amenities. Even amidst the Great Depression, Ackerman's photographs continued in this optimistic vein, one that contrasts sharply with the grim images of rural poverty taken by other Federal photographers. He later recalled that he tried "to paint the rural scene as I saw it, modern and up-to-date in many respects."

George Ackerman's photographic prints and many of his original negatives can be found among the records of several Federal agricultural agencies, most notably the records of the Office of the Secretary of Agriculture and of the Extension Service. ■

60 **Customer at Auburn Savings Bank**
By George W. Ackerman, Auburn, Maine,
1929
National Archives and Records Administration,
Records of the Extension Service
(33-SC-12790c)

61 "Negro family budget of canned fruits and vegetables. (Mr. and Mrs. J.E. Bryan) expert canners in their community."
By George W. Ackerman, Robeson County, North Carolina, May 20, 1932
National Archives and Records Administration, Records of the Extension Service (33-SC-15906c)

62 *Opposite:* "Unloading dry farm wheat"
By George W. Ackerman, Washington, 1925
National Archives and Records Administration,
Records of the Extension Service
(33-SC-5094c)

63 "Postman delivering mail, rural mail
route, York county, Maine"
By George W. Ackerman, August 26, 1930
National Archives and Records Administration,
Records of the Extension Service
(33-SC-14560c)

66 **"One-Third of a Nation"**
By Arnold Eagle and David Robbins,
1938
*National Archives and Records
Administration, Records of the Work
Projects Administration*
(69-ANP-1-2329-214)

64 *Opposite:* **Hoover (Boulder) Dam
project**
By an unknown photographer for
the Bureau of Reclamation, ca. 1934
*Herbert Hoover Library, National Archives
and Records Administration*
(1934-79A)

65 **Civilian Conservation Corps
workforce in Yosemite National Park**
By an unknown photographer,
Yosemite National Park, California,
ca. June–December 1935
*National Archives and Records
Administration–Pacific Region (San
Francisco), Records of the National
Park Service*

67 United Auto Workers' sit-down strike, Flint, Michigan. Strikers seized the General Motors plant for 6 weeks in January and February 1937.
By Sheldon Dick
Franklin D. Roosevelt Library, National Archives and Records Administration
(71-93)

68 "Bonus Marchers" and police battle in Washington, DC. The marchers came to Washington, DC, to demand from Congress the immediate payment of their military pension "bonuses." After several months of camping near the Anacostia River, and a series of confrontations with the police, the marchers were driven from the city by Federal troops.
By the Associated Press, July 1932
National Archives and Records Administration, Records of the Office of the Chief Signal Officer
(111-SC-97560)

69 "2603 Co. Civilian Conservation Corps, Camp
Vermillion, Danville, Ill[inois]. Boxing team.
Mr. Taylor, trainer."
By an unknown photographer, 1936–39
National Archives and Records Administration,
Records of the Civilian Conservation Corps
(35-GC-VI-219-D3)

70 "Commercialized entertainment in the village is confined to the movie house, which has films only once every two weeks, and the pool hall, which is looked down upon by many of the community's most substantial citizens. Nevertheless, there are generally a few players to be seen here in the evenings and a particularly large group on Saturday night."
By Irving Rusinow, ca. April 10–16, 1941
National Archives and Records Administration, Records of the Bureau of Agricultural Economics
(83-G-44220)

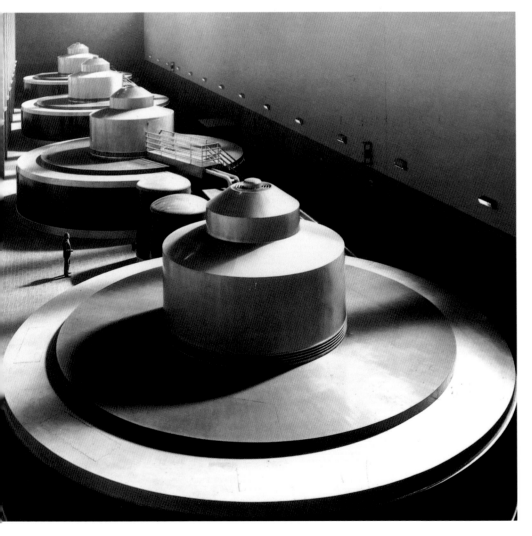

71 "The Pickwick Dam powerhouse contains four generators with a capacity of 144,000 kilowatts. Two additional units are scheduled for the plant which will bring the total to 216,000 kw. All T[ennessee] V[alley] A[uthority] installations are linked into a single system through a network of transmission lines."
By an unknown photographer, Tennessee, not dated
National Archives and Records Administration–Southeast Region, Records of the Tennessee Valley Authority

72 "This man is descended from one of the oldest families in the village, and his house is also one of the oldest there. El Cerrito, San Miguel County, New Mexico."
By Irving Rusinow, ca. April 10–16, 1941
National Archives and Records Administration, Records of the Bureau of Agricultural Economics
(83-G-3782

73 "Street corner next to Federal Building where U.S. Dept. of Labor handles naturalization of immigrants"
By an unknown photographer, New York, New York, 1939
National Archives and Records Administration, Records of the National Youth Administration
(119-G-81-M-29)

74 "On the freights. He said he quit
high school after two years, hung around
home for a couple of years, and then got
work as general kitchen help in a hotel.
He had just been fired from a job of
this kind in Los Angeles where he had
'blown up' and 'told the cook off.' He
carried a clean white shirt and was
prepared to look for work when his
money was completely gone. 'I don't
know where I'll go. Huntin' for a job I
guess. I didn't go home—I'm on the
bum. These agency jobs; you gotta buy
them and I ain't got the dough.' He
talked about going to Redding, to
Eugene, and to Seattle. He had $1.80.
Youba County, California."
By Rondal Partridge, April 13, 1940
National Archives and Records Administration,
Records of the National
Youth Administration
(119-CAL-13)

75 "Children and Sugar Beets"
By L.C. Harmon, Hall County, Nebraska,
October 17, 1940
National Archives and Records Administration,
Records of the Office of the Secretary of Agriculture
(16-G-159-AAA-6437W)

76 "Abandoned house, Haskell County,
Kansas"
By Irving Rusinow, April 1941
National Archives and Records Administration,
Records of the Bureau of Agricultural Economics
(83-G-41906)

77 President Franklin D. Roosevelt with his
dog Fala and Ruthie Bie, granddaughter of
a gardener who worked for the Roosevelt
family, at Top Cottage. This rare photograph
is one of only two known showing President
Roosevelt in his wheelchair.
By Margaret Suckley, Hyde Park, New York,
February 1941
Franklin D. Roosevelt Library, National Archives
and Records Administration

79 **"New York, N.Y.: Harlem street scene, showing shopping district"**
By an unknown photographer, ca. 1942
National Archives and Records Administration, Records of the U.S. Information Agency
(306-PS-50-4743)

80 *Opposite:* **"Gerald Nailor, Navajo Artist"**
By Milton Snow, Window Rock, Arizona, August 1943
National Archives and Records Administration, Records of the Bureau of Indian Affairs
(75-NG-NC-2-14)

78 Orson Welles appearing in the Works Progress Administration's Theatre Project production of *Doctor Faustus*
By an unknown photographer, New York, New York, 1937
National Archives and Records Administration, Records of the Work Projects Administration
(119-G-81-M-29)

DOROTHEA LANGE

Born in Hoboken, New Jersey, Dorothea Lange (1895–1965) announced her intention to become a photographer at age 18. After apprenticing with a photographer in New York City, she moved to San Francisco and in 1919 established her own studio. During the 1920s and early 1930s, Lange worked as a portrait photographer, usually for San Francisco's upper classes. But by 1932, wanting to see a world different from the society families she had been photographing, Lange began shooting San Francisco's urban unemployed and labor unrest. In 1933 she photographed the most famous of these images at the White Angel Jungle, a soup kitchen for San Francisco's jobless.

The photographs she took at the White Angel and elsewhere over the next few months changed the direction of Lange's photography. In 1935 she accepted a position as a staff photographer with the Federal Resettlement Administration (RA), later renamed the Farm Security Administration (FSA). Her work for the RA/FSA took Lange to the South, where she documented small towns, the lives of tenant farmers, and experimental agricultural communities. Returning to the West, she focused on the lives of migrant workers. In 1940 she was hired by the Bureau of Agricultural Economics (BAE) to produce photographs for a series of community studies in California and Arizona. During World War II, Lange photographed the internment of Japanese Americans for the War Relocation Authority (WRA) and the Kaiser shipyards in Richmond, California for the Office of War Information (OWI). After the war, despite ill health, she photographed the founding of the United Nations for the State Department and completed several assignments for Life Magazine in the United States and around the world.

81 *Opposite:* "**White Angel Breadline**"
By Dorothea Lange, San Francisco, California, 1933
National Archives and Records Administration, Records of the Social Security Administration
(47-GA-90-497)

82 "**Young migratory mother, originally from Texas. On the day before the photograph was made she and her husband traveled 35 miles each way to pick peas. They worked 5 hours each and together earned $2.25. They have two young children . . . Live in auto camp.**"
By Dorothea Lange, Edison County, California, April 11, 1940
National Archives and Records Administration, Records of the Bureau of Agricultural Economics
(83-G-41543)

Dorothea Lange's photographs in the National Archives include prints and negatives of her work for the BAE as well as prints and original negatives of her work for the WRA. In addition, there are a small number of prints from her FSA and OWI assignments, the bulk of which are now held by the Library of Congress and other repositories. ■

83 "Between Weedpatch and Lamont, Kern County, California. Children living in camp."
By Dorothea Lange, April 20, 1940
National Archives and Records Administration, Records of the Bureau of Agricultural Economics
(83-G-41456)

84 "Members of the Mochida family await-
ing evacuation bus. Identification tags were
used to aid in keeping a family unit intact
during all phases of evacuation. Mochida
operated a nursery and five greenhouses
on a two-acre site in Eden Township."
By Dorothea Lange, Hayward, California,
May 8, 1942
National Archives and Records Administration,
Records of the War Relocation Authority
(210-GC-153)

85 "Cheap Auto Camp Housing for
Citrus Workers"
By Dorothea Lange, Tulare County, California,
February 1940
National Archives and Records Administration,
Records of the Bureau of Agricultural Economics
(83-G-41555)

ANSEL ADAMS

Ansel Adams (1902–1984) is one of the most celebrated photographers of all time. His images of the American landscape, and especially those of the American West, are familiar to millions. Born and raised in San Francisco, Adams studied music as a youth with the hope of becoming a concert pianist. At age 14, while on a family vacation, he took his first snapshots of Yosemite National Park. From that time on, Adams was captivated by the idea of recording nature on film. While in his twenties, he abandoned his musical ambitions for a career in photography, working as a portrait and commercial photographer. By the 1930s he began to achieve success for his visionary yet highly detailed photographs of western landscapes, especially those taken in Yosemite National Park. Over the next decades, Adams continued to work as a photographer, staging exhibitions and writing several important books on photographic technique. He also became a champion of the conservation movement in the United States, speaking out for environmental concerns and serving on the board of directors of the Sierra Club. Today, Ansel Adams's photographs remain immensely popular, "conveying to millions a vision of an ideal America where nature's grand scenes and gentle details live on in undiminished glory."

In 1941 Secretary of the Interior Harold Ickes asked Adams to take photographs of the American West for a series of murals to be installed in the Department of the Interior Building in Washington, DC. The murals were never completed, but 226 of Adams's signed original prints were later added to the National Archives holdings and can be found among the Records of the National Park Service. ■

86 *Opposite:* **"Church, Taos Pueblo, New Mex, 1942"**
By Ansel Adams
National Archives and Records Administration, Records of the National Park Service
(79-AAQ-1)

87 **"Grand Canyon from South Rim, 1941, Arizona"**
By Ansel Adams
National Archives and Records Administration, Records of the National Park Service
(79-AAF-8)

88 "The Tetons—Snake River"
By Ansel Adams, 1942
National Archives and Records Administration,
Records of the National Park Service
(79-AAG-1)

89 "In Glacier National Park"
By Ansel Adams, 1941
National Archives and Records Administration,
Records of the National Park Service
(79-AAE-23)

92 "An American armored vehicle blasts Nazis fleeing St. Lo and moves on into the city in the face of concentrated artillery fire. The intensity of the battery can be seen in the empty shell casings tossed in the road."
By Witscher, July 20, 1944
National Archives and Records Administration, Records of the Office of the Chief Signal Officer (111-SC-191876)

93 "Landing on the coast of France under heavy Nazi machine gun fire are these American soldiers, shown just as they left the ramp of a Coast Guard landing boat."
By CphoM. Robert F. Sargent, June 6, 1944
National Archives and Records Administration, Records of the U.S. Coast Guard (26-G-2343)

90 *Opposite:* "Coast Guardsmen on the deck of the U.S. Coast Guard Cutter *Spencer* watch the explosion of a depth charge which blasted a Nazi U-boat's hope of breaking into the center of a large convoy. Sinking of U–175."
By Warrant Officer Jack, January, April 17, 1943
National Archives and Records Administration, Records of the U.S. Coast Guard (26-G-1517)

91 "USS *Shaw* (DD–373) exploding during the Japanese raid on Pearl Harbor"
By an unknown photographer, December 7, 1941
National Archives and Records Administration, General Records of the Department of the Navy, 1798–1947 (80-G-16871)

94 "Burial at sea for the officers and men of the USS *Intrepid* (CV–11) who lost their lives when the carrier was hit by Japanese bombs during operations in the Philippines."
By Lt. Barrett Gallagher, November 26, 1944
National Archives and Records Administration, General Records of the Department of the Navy, 1798–1947
(80-G-468912)

95 "Sprawled bodies on beach of Tarawa, testifying to ferocity of the struggle for this stretch of sand."
By an unknown photographer, November 1943
National Archives and Records Administration, General Records of the Department of the Navy, 1798–1947
(80-G-57405)

96 "Pilots pleased over their victory during the Marshall Islands attack, grin across the tail of an F6F Hellcat on board the U.S.S. *Lexington*, after shooting down 17 out of 20 Japanese planes heading for Tarawa."
By Comdr. Edward J. Steichen, November 1943
National Archives and Records Administration, General Records of the Department of the Navy, 1798–1947
(80-G-470985)

97 "U.S. Marine in action at Peleliu Island, Palau Islands"
By an unknown photographer, September 1944
National Archives and Records Administration, General Records of the Department of the Navy, 1798–1947
(80-G-48358)

98 *Opposite:* "Cpl. Carlton Chapman . . .
is a machine-gunner in an M–4 tank,
attached to a Motor Transport unit near
Nancy, France."
By Ryan, November 5, 1944
National Archives and Records Administration,
Records of the Office of the Chief Signal Officer
(111-SC-196106)

99 "Standing between advancing U.S.
Seventh Army troops, an old German
woman, in despair, surveys the hopeless
wreckage of her home. 1st Battalion,
180th Inf. Reg., 45th Division.
Bensheim, Germany."
By an unknown photographer, March 27,
1945
National Archives and Records Administration,
Records of the Office of the Chief Signal Officer
(111-SC-204729)

100 **Destroyed U.S. Flying Fortress**
By an unknown photographer, ca.
1942–45
National Archives and Records
Administration, Records of the Office of War
Information
(208-YE-142)

101 "Typical of the thousands of young Negro women summoned to Washington, DC, for war work, Miss Clara Camlillo Carroll of Cleveland O., arrives in the Union Station in the Nation's Capital to accept an appointment as clerk in the mail and files section of the Ordinance Department of the War Department. It was a cold and dreary morning when Miss Carroll arrived."
By Roger Smith, 1943
National Archives and Records Administration, Records of the Office of War Information
(208-NP-3F-4)

104 "Building the SS *Frederick Douglass* in Baltimore, MD. More than 6,000 Negro shipyard workers are employed at the Bethlehem-Fairfield Shipyard where the Liberty Ship, SS *Frederick Douglass*, is being rushed to completion. The noted orator and abolitionist leader worked as a ship caulker in the vicinity of this yard before he escaped from slavery. Welders S.L. Ramsey and Benny Chen (Chinese) on aft end of flat keel."
By Roger Smith, ca. 1943
National Archives and Records Administration,
Records of the Office of War Information
(208-NP-1DDD-5)

102 *Opposite:* "Mechanical crew at the Baton Rouge Esso Refinery in line for their pay checks"
By Edwin Rosskam, December 1943
National Archives and Records Administration,
Records of the Office of War Information
(208-LO-14F-27)

103 "With nearly 1,000 Negro women employed as burners, welders, scalers and in other capacities at the Kaiser Shipyards in Richmond, Calif., women war workers played an important part in the construction of the Liberty Ship, SS *George Washington Carver*, launched on May 7, 1943. Miss Eastine Crowner, a former waitress, is shown at her job as a scaler."
By E.F. Joseph, 1943
National Archives and Records Administration,
Records of the Office of War Information
(208-NP-2GGG-1)

106 "Starving inmate of Camp Gusen, Austria"
By T4c. Sam Gilbert, May 12, 1945
National Archives and Records Administration,
Records of the Office of the Chief Signal Officer
(111-SC-264918)

107 *Opposite:* "American servicemen and women gather in front of 'Rainbow Corner' Red Cross club in Paris to celebrate the unconditional surrender of the Japanese."
By McNulty, August 15, 1945
National Archives and Records Administration,
Records of the Office of the Chief Signal Officer
(111-SC-210241)

105 "A few of the thousands of wedding rings the Germans removed from their victims to salvage the gold. U.S. troops found rings, watches, precious stones, eyeglasses, and gold fillings, near Buchenwald concentration camp."
By T4c. Roberts, May 5, 1945
National Archives and Records Administration,
Records of the Office of the Chief Signal Officer
(111-SC-206406)

CHARLES FENNO JACOBS

Shortly after the Japanese attack on Pearl Harbor, famed photographer Edward Steichen recruited Charles Fenno Jacobs (1904–1975) to join his Naval Aviation Photographic Unit. The U.S. Navy had established this special group to document and publicize its aviation activities and allowed Steichen to recruit the most talented photographers he could find. By 1941 Jacobs had already established a reputation as a photographer, having worked for *Life*, *Fortune*, and *U.S. Camera* magazines and briefly for the Farm Security Administration.

Jacobs, like the other photographers in the Naval Aviation Photographic Unit, followed Steichen's advice to concentrate on the human side of modern war. He photographed aircraft workers in California, capturing the then-novel sight of female factory workers. On another assignment he photographed life aboard the battleship U.S.S. *New Jersey*, shooting the crew off as well as on duty. Other of Jacobs's images capture the earnestness of young aviation cadets, the humiliation of a Japanese prisoner of war, and melancholy scenes of Navy pilots on leave with their dates.

When the war ended, Jacobs and two of his colleagues, still dressed in uniforms, walked into the offices of *Fortune* and boldly proposed that the magazine hire them, and assign each a different part of the world as his beat. The magazine agreed and Jacobs was assigned to cover Europe in the immediate postwar years.

Prints of Fenno Jacobs's photographs and many of his original negatives are found in the National Archives among the General Records of the United States Navy, 1789–1946. ∎

108 *Opposite:* "**Man working on hull of U.S. Submarine at Electric Boat Co., Groton, Conn.**"
By Lt. Comdr. Charles Fenno Jacobs, August 1943
National Archives and Records Administration, General Records of the Department of the Navy, 1798–1947
(80-G-468517)

109 "**Navy pilots on leave dancing with their dates at the Chris Holmes Rest Home in Hawaii**"
By Lt. Comdr. Charles Fenno Jacobs, March 1944
National Archives and Records Administration, General Records of the Department of the Navy, 1798–1947
(80-G-475095)

111 "Lunch time at the Vega aircraft plant, Burbank, Calif. A quartet of girl workers."
By Lt. Comdr. Charles Fenno Jacobs, August 1943
National Archives and Records Administration, General Records of the Department of the Navy, 1798–1947
(80-G-412639)

112 *Opposite:* "Much tattooed sailor aboard the USS *New Jersey* (BB 62)"
By Lt. Comdr. Charles Fenno Jacobs, December 1944
National Archives and Records Administration, General Records of the Department of the Navy, 1798–1947
(80-G-470222)

110 "Japanese prisoners of war are bathed, clipped, 'deloused,' and issued GI clothing as soon as they are taken aboard the USS *New Jersey*."
By Lt. Comdr. Charles Fenno Jacobs, December 1944
National Archives and Records Administration, General Records of the Department of the Navy, 1798–1947
(80-G-469956)

113 *Opposite:* "Chicago Ill. Looking down Michigan Avenue in Chicago. Buildings shown are (L. to R.) #333 No. Michigan Avenue; Carbon and Carbide Building; London Guarantee & Accident Building; Lincoln Tower; Pure Oil; and Wrigley Building"
By Oliver E. Pfeiffer, March 1951
National Archives and Records Administration, Records of the U.S. Information Agency
(306-PS-51-4723)

114 **President Harry Truman and Secret Service agents on a walk near the White House**
By Harris and Ewing, Washington, DC, 1946
Harry S. Truman Library, National Archives and Records Administration
(59-898)

115 "Saturday afternoon street scene"
By Russell Lee, Welch, West Virginia, August 24, 1946
National Archives and Records Administration, Records of the Solid Fuels Administration for War
(245-MS-1942L)

116 "Mrs. John Whitehead, wife of miner, and two of her children (or grandchildren) in the kitchen of her three room house. Mr. and Mrs. John Whitehead and their six children and six grandchildren live here. This house, built on company owned land, was built by Mrs. Whitehead's half brother at no expense for materials or labor to the company; the builder (half brother) was to receive the use of the house rent-free for three years and at the end of this period the ownership of the house would revert to the company. The brother moved away at the end of one year, receiving no cash settlement from the company. The house now rents for $6 monthly. It has no running water, no electricity, access is over a mountain trail; there are three rooms."

By Russell Lee, Field, Kentucky, August 31, 1946

National Archives and Records Administration, Records of the Solid Fuels Administration for War

(245-MS-2134)

117 *Top Corner:* "Interior of modern kitchen which has U-shaped arrangement for easy access to all work areas. Electric stove is at left, electric refrigerator is at right with steel sink and work space between. Electric dishwasher is in compartment to right of sink."
By Westinghouse Electric Corporation, ca. 1950
National Archives and Records Administration, Records of the U.S. Information Agency
(3-6-PS-50-726)

118 "Levittown, Pennsylvania. An aerial view of the famous housing project."
By Ed Latcham, ca. 1959
National Archives and Records Administration, Records of the U.S. Information Agency
(306-PS-59-13580)

119 "Vienna, VA. James S. Thomas and family viewing television in the living room of their home." From the pamphlet *Television—Promise and Problem.*
By Everet F. Bumgardner, ca. 1958
National Archives and Records Administration, Records of the U.S. Information Agency
(306-PS-58-9015)

120 "Men of the 1st Marine Division capture Chinese Communists during fighting on the central Korean front. Hoengsong."

By Pfc. C.T. Wehner, March 2, 1951
National Archives and Records Administration, Records of the U.S. Marine Corps
(127-N-A6759)

121 "'Exercise Desert Rock.' Troops of the Battalion Combat Team, U.S. Army 11th Airborne Division, watch a plume of radio-active smoke rise after a D-Day blast at Yucca Flats, as the much prepared Exercise 'Desert Rock' reaches its peak."

By Corporal McCaughey, Las Vegas, Nevada, November 1, 1951
National Archives and Records Administration, Records of the Office of the Chief Signal Officer
(111-SC-389297)

122 "A grief stricken American infantryman whose buddy has been killed in action
is comforted by another soldier. In the background a corpsman methodically fills
out casualty tags, Haktong-ni area Korea."
By Sfc. Al Chang, August 28, 1950
National Archives and Records Administration, Records of the Office of the Chief Signal Officer
(111-SC-347803)

123 **A birthday party for David Eisenhower, grandson of President Dwight Eisenhower. In attendance were movie and television stars Roy Rogers and Dale Evans.**
By Abbey Rowe, Washington, DC, March 31, 1956
Dwight D. Eisenhower Library, National Archives and Records Administration
(62-187)

124 "VIPs view DOG detonation from Officers Beach Club patio (lawn chair observers)."
By an unknown photographer, Enewetak Island, April 7, 1951
National Archives and Records Administration, Records of the Defense Nuclear Agency
(374-ANT-20-PL-19-03)

125 "Fallout shelter built by Louis Severance adjacent to his home near Akron, Mich., includes a special ventilation and escape hatch, an entrance to his basement, tiny kitchen, running water, sanitary facilities, and a sleeping and living area for the family of four. The shelter cost about $1,000. It has a 10-inch reinforced concrete ceiling with thick earth cover and concrete walls. Severance says, 'Ever since I was convinced what damage H-Bombs can do, I've wanted to build the shelter. Just as with my chicken farm, when there's a need I build it.'"
By an unknown photographer, ca. 1960
National Archives and Records Administration, Records of the Defense Civil Preparedness Agency
(397-MA-2s-160)

126 A young demonstrator at the March on Washington for Jobs and Freedom
By an unknown photographer, Washington, DC, August 28, 1963
National Archives and Records Administration, Records of the U.S. Information Agency
(306-SSM-4B-61-32)

127 "Little Rock, Arkansas: Negroes leave segregated Baptist church entrance after deacons explained that the minister was on their side but their effort to enter would disrupt services."
By an unknown photographer, October 5, 1958
National Archives and Records Administration, Records of the U.S. Information Agency
(306-PSC-63-4119)
©AP/WideWorld Photos

128 **President John F. Kennedy with his son, John, Jr., on the beach at Newport, Rhode Island**
By Robert L. Knudsen, September 12, 1963
John F. Kennedy Library, National Archives and Records Administration
(KN-C-30007)

129 **Lyndon Johnson takes the Presidential oath of office aboard** *Air Force One* **after the assassination of President John F. Kennedy.**
By Cecil Stoughton, Dallas, Texas, November 22, 1963
Lyndon Baines Johnson Library, National Archives and Records Administration

YOICHI OKAMOTO

Born in Yonkers, New York, Yoichi Okamoto (1915–85) was educated at Colgate University. After serving as a still- and motion-picture photographer in the U.S. Army in World War II, he headed the Army's Signal Corps's photo office in occupied Austria and then worked briefly as a photographer for a Syracuse, New York, newspaper. Okamoto then joined the United States Information Agency (USIA) serving as staff photographer in USIA posts in Germany and Austria, and eventually as chief of the Visual Materials Branch in Washington, DC. Two of his photographs were chosen for the landmark 1955 photography exhibition "The Family of Man." In 1961 Okamoto accompanied Vice President Lyndon Johnson on a visit to West Berlin. Johnson was so pleased with Okamoto's work that he asked him to join him on several other trips. When Johnson became President, he appointed Okamoto White House photographer. After President Johnson left office in 1969, Okamoto founded a custom photo laboratory in Washington, DC, and continued to work as a freelance photographer.

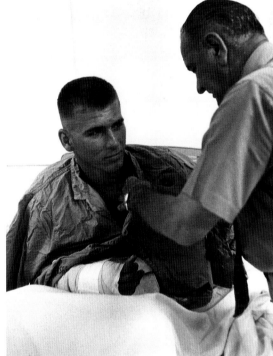

130 *Opposite:* **Rev. Martin Luther King, Jr. President Lyndon Johnson can be seen in the background.**
By Yoichi Okamoto, the White House, Washington, DC, March 18, 1966
Lyndon Baines Johnson Library, National Archives and Records Administration
(A2133-10)

131 **President Lyndon Johnson awards a medal to a wounded U.S. serviceman in Cam Rahn Bay, South Vietnam.**
By Yoichi Okamoto, October 26, 1966
Lyndon Baines Johnson Library, National Archives and Records Administration
(A3395-5)

Yoichi Okamoto's photography reveals a gift for capturing his subject's personality. This is especially true of his work as White House photographer, where he gained unprecedented access to Lyndon Johnson. Okamoto was able to grasp Johnson's changeable moods, and his candid images tell us much about LBJ's personal political style. His goal, he told Johnson, was not just to take portraits but "to hang around and try to document history in the making." In his other Government work, Okamoto demonstrated a strong appreciation for setting and context. His images of Washington, DC; Munich, Germany; and other cities, for example, show us the joys and irritations of urban life.

Yoichi Okamoto's photography is well represented in the holdings of the National Archives. In addition to his White House photographs, at the Lyndon Baines Johnson Library in Austin, Texas, his work as a USIA staff member as well as some of his later free lance photographs can be found throughout USIA photographic files. In 1973 Okamoto completed several assignments for the Environmental Protection Agency's DOCUMERICA project. These photographs along with Okamoto's captions and some of his letters are also found in the National Archives. ■

132 **Senator Robert F. Kennedy and his aide Theodore Sorenson**
By Yoichi Okamoto, the White House, Washington, DC, April 3, 1968
Lyndon Baines Johnson Library, National Archives and Records Administration
(A5993-23a)

133 *Opposite:* **President Lyndon Johnson meets with Presidential candidate Richard Nixon at the White House.**
By Yoichi Okamoto, July 26, 1968
Lyndon Baines Johnson Library, National Archives and Records Administration
(D1202-15)

134 "Street arrest"
By Yoichi Okamoto, Washington, DC, May 1973
National Archives and Records Administration, Records of the Environmental Protection Agency
(412-DA-4146)

135 *Opposite:* "SP4 Ruediger Richter (Columbus, Georgia), 4th Bn., 503 Inf., 173 Abn Bde (Separate), lifts his battle weary eyes to the heavens, as if to ask why? SGT. Daniel E. Spencer (Bend, Oregon) stares down at their fallen comrade. The day's battle ended, they silently await the helicopter which will evacuate their comrade from the jungle covered hills in Long Khanh Province."
By Pfc. L. Paul Epley, 1966
National Archives and Records Administration, Records of the Office of the Chief Signal Officer (111-SC-635974)

136 "Da Nang, Vietnam . . . A young Marine private waits on the beach during the Marine landing."
By an unknown photographer, August 3, 1965
National Archives and Records Administration, Records of the U.S. Marine Corps (127-N-A-185146)

137 President Lyndon Johnson listens to a tape recording from his son-in-law Capt. Charles Robb, a Marine Corps company commander in Vietnam.
By Jack Kightlinger, Washington, DC, July 31, 1968
Lyndon Baines Johnson Library, National Archives and Records Administration (B1274-1b)

138 "Helicopters of the 170th and the 189th Helicopter Assault Companies await the loading of troops at Polei Kleng, in the Central Highlands of the Republic of South Vietnam."
By Spc. Thomas Lykens, April 10, 1969
National Archives and Records Administration, Records of the Office of the Chief Signal Officer (111-SC-651778)

139 "A female demonstrator offers a
flower to military police on guard at the
Pentagon during an anti-Vietnam
demonstration."
By S. Sgt. Albert R. Simpson, Arlington,
Virginia, October 21, 1967
National Archives and Records Administration,
Records of the Office of the Chief Signal Officer
(111-CC-46331)

140 **Aftermath of the Detroit, Michigan,**
riots
By an unknown photographer, July 1967
National Archives and Records Administration,
Records of ACTION
(362-VS-3F-5999-13)

141 *Opposite:* "**Close-up view of an astronaut's leg and foot and foot-print in the lunar soil, photographed with a 70mm lunar surface camera during the Apollo 11 lunar surface extravehicular activity. Astronaut Michael Collins, command module pilot remained with the Command Service Modules in lunar orbit while astronauts Neil A. Armstrong, commander, and Edwin E. Aldrin, Jr., lunar module pilot, explored the Moon.**"
By Neil Armstrong, July 20, 1969
National Archives and Records Administration,
Records of the U.S. Information Agency
(306-PSD-69-3133c)

142 "**Rising earth greets Apollo VIII astronauts as they come from behind the moon after the lunar orbit insertion burn. Earth is about 5 degrees above the horizon.**"
By William Anders, December 29, 1968
National Archives and Records Administration,
Records of the U.S. Information Agency
(306-PSD-68-4049c)

144 "Hanoi, North Vietnam . . . American servicemen, former prisoners of war, are cheering as their aircraft takes off from an airfield near Hanoi as part of Operation Homecoming."
By an unknown photographer, February 1973
National Archives and Records Administration, Records of the U.S. Marine Corps
(127-N-A900056)

143 **President Richard Nixon visits the Great Wall during his trip to China.**
By Oliver F. Atkins, February 24, 1972
Nixon Presidential Materials Project, National Archives and Records Administration
(C8566-21A)

145 "South China Sea . . . Crewmen of the amphibious cargo ship U.S.S. *Durham* (LKA-114) take Vietnamese refugees aboard from a small craft. The refugees will be transferred later by mechanized landing craft (LCM) to the freighter *Transcolorado*."
By JO1 Mike McGougan, April 3, 1975
National Archives and Records Administration, General Records of the Department of the Navy, 1947–
(428-K-108890)

146 "Housing Adjacent to U.S. Steel Plant"
By Leroy Woodson, Birmingham, Alabama,
July 1972
National Archives and Records Administration,
Records of the Environmental Protection Agency
(412-DA-2911)

147 *Opposite:* **Richard Nixon departs from the**
White House after Gerald Ford was sworn in
as President.
By Oliver F. Atkins, Washington, DC, August 9, 1974
Nixon Presidential Materials Project, National Archives
and Records Administration
(E3398-09)

148 **"Taking shelter during a dust storm"**
By Terry Eiler, Four Corners area, Utah, May
1972
National Archives and Records Administration,
Records of the Environmental Protection Agency
(412-DA-1834)

149 "New Jersey Flats near
Hoboken, with Statue of
Liberty in background"
By Dan McCoy, August 1973
National Archives and Records Administration,
Records of the Environmental Protection
Agency
(412-DA-11898)

150 President Gerald Ford
campaigns in Walnut Creek, California.
By David Hume Kennerly, May 26, 1976
Gerald R. Ford Library, National Archives and
Records Administration
(A9971-27)

151 President Jimmy Carter and daughter Amy running to *Marine One*
By Jack Kightlinger, Washington, DC,
May 13, 1977
*Jimmy Carter Library, National Archives and
Records Administration*
(C123-13A)

**152 "Gas stations abandoned during the
fuel crisis in the winter of 1973–74 were
sometimes used for other purposes. This
station at Potlatch, Washington, west of
Olympia was turned into a religious
meeting hall. Signs painted on the gas
pumps proclaim 'fill up with the Holy
Ghost . . . and Salvation.'"**
By David Falconer, April 1974
*National Archives and Records Administration,
Records of the Environmental Protection Agency*
(412-DA-13061)

153 **Vice President George Bush at the opening of Martin Luther King Holiday Commission**
By Gerald Dean, Washington, DC 1985
National Archives and Records Administration, General Records of the Department of Housing and Urban Development
(207-N6134-5-18A)

154 *Opposite:* **"President Reagan speaking at a rally for Senator Durenberger"**
By Michael Evans, February 8, 1982
Ronald Reagan Library, National Archives and Records Administration
(C6289-25)

155 "Religious fervor is mirrored on the face of a Black Muslim woman, one of some 10,000 listening to Elijah Muhammad deliver his annual Savior's Day message in Chicago. The city is headquarters for the Black Muslims. Their $75 million dollar empire includes a mosque, newspaper, university, restaurants, real estate, bank, and variety of retail stores. Muhammad died February 25, 1975."
By John H. White, March 1974
National Archives and Records Administration, Records of the Environmental Protection Agency (412-DA-13792)

156 "Scenes of the Space Shuttle *Challenger* taken with a 70mm camera onboard the shuttle pallet satellite (SPAS–01)."
By a *Challenger* crew member, June 22, 1983
National Archives and Records Administration, Records of the U.S. Information Agency
(306-PSE-83-2622/cA)

157 "President Bill Clinton plays the saxophone presented to him by Russian President Boris Yeltsin at a private dinner hosted by President Yeltsin at Novoya Ogarova Dacha, Russia."
By Bob McNeeley, January 13, 1994
Courtesy of the White House
(P011471-26A)

158 "First Ladies Nancy Reagan, Ladybird Johnson, Hillary Rodham Clinton, Rosalyn Carter, Betty Ford, and Barbara Bush sit together at the National Garden Gala, 'A Tribute to America's First Ladies.'"
By Barbara Kinney, U.S. Botanic Garden, Washington, DC, May 11, 1994
Courtesy of the White House
(P015515-28)

DANNY LYON

Danny Lyon (1942–) is one of the most original documentary photographers of the late 20th century. Lyon grew up in a middle-class section of New York City and began to make photographs at the age of 17. He studied history at the University of Chicago and in 1962 joined the civil rights movement, becoming staff photographer for the Student Nonviolent Coordinating Committee (SNCC). His SNCC photographs are powerful, behind-the-scenes views of the struggle for racial equality; they depict the courage and idealism of those in the movement as well as the hatred and violence employed by segregationists. During the next three decades, Lyon's photography concentrated on the lives of the poor, ignored, and disenfranchised. He photographed motorcycle gang members, inmates in Texas penitentiaries, and demolition derby drivers. He documented the destruction of Lower Manhattan through urban renewal, a revolution in Haiti, and life in inner city Brooklyn. In 1969 Lyon began making films, which include *Llanito*, *Little Boy*, and *Willie*.

Lyon worked sporadically for the Federal Government as a photographer from 1972 through 1974, completing several assignments for the Environmental Protection Agency's DOCUMERICA project. In 1972–1973 he photographed the Rio Grande Valley and the Chicano barrio of South El Paso, Texas, as well as Galveston, and Houston, Texas. In 1974 he photographed the Bedford-Stuyvesant section of Brooklyn, New York. Lyon's images from these assignments mirror the concerns of his non-Governmental work. They depict ethnic neighborhoods under attack by outside forces, including Federally driven policies such as urban renewal. His photographs sought to preserve and record these communities before they were destroyed. That Lyon felt free to criticize the very Government that was employing him says a great deal about the freedom given to DOCUMERICA photographers.

Danny Lyon's original 35 mm color slides from the DOCUMERICA project, along with supporting written materials, are preserved at the National Archives among the records of the Environmental Protection Agency. ■

159 *Opposite:* "**Chicano teenager in El Paso's second ward. A classic barrio which is slowly giving way to urban renewal.**"
By Danny Lyon, South El Paso, Texas, July 1972
National Archives and Records Administration, Records of the Environmental Protection Agency (412-DA-2822)

160 "**Grave marker in Smelter cemetery, Asarco Smelter Works, in the background. This is the graveyard provided for employees.**"
By Danny Lyon, South El Paso, Texas, July 1972
National Archives and Records Administration, Records of the Environmental Protection Agency (412-DA-2821)

161 "Automobile in second ward, El Paso's Chicano neighborhood. South El Paso, Texas."
By Danny Lyon, June 1972
National Archives and Records Administration, Records of the Environmental Protection Agency (412-DA-2842)

162 "Three boys and 'A Train' graffiti in Brooklyn's Lynch Park in New York City. The inner city today is an absolute contradiction to the main stream America of gas stations, expressways, and tract homes. It is populated by Blacks, Latins, and the white poor. Most of all the inner city environment is human beings as beautiful and threatened as the 19th century buildings."
By Danny Lyon, Brooklyn, New York, New York, July 1974
National Archives and Records Administration, Records of the Environmental Protection Agency (412-DA-13449)

163 "Boy against a yellow platform at the Kosciusko Swimming Pool in the Bedford-Stuyvesant District of Brooklyn in New York City. Inner city residents enjoy themselves at this intelligently located pool. The inner city today is an absolute contradiction to the main stream America of gas stations, expressways, shopping centers, and tract homes. It is populated by Blacks, Latins, and the white poor."

By Danny Lyon, New York, New York, July 1974

National Archives and Records Administration, Records of the Environmental Protection Agency

(412-DA-13474)

For Further Reading

20th Century History

Barbeau, Arthur, and Henri Florette. *The Unknown Soldier: Black American Troops in World War I* . Philadelphia: Temple University Press, 1979.

Carroll, Peter. *It Seemed Like Nothing Happened: The Tragedy and Promise of American Life in the 1970s.* New Brunswick: Rutgers University Press, 1990

Cashman, Sean Dennis. *America in the Age of Titans: The Progressive Era and World War I.* New York: New York University Press, 1988.

Chambers, John Whiteclay, III. *The Tyranny of Change: America in the Progressive Era, 1900–1917.* New York: St. Martin's Press, 1980.

Hawley, Ellis W. *The Great War and the Search for a Modern Order.* New York: St. Martin's Press, 1979.

Hixson, Walter. *Parting the Curtin: Propaganda, Culture, and the Cold War, 1945–1961.* New York: St. Martin's Press, 1997.

Hodgson, Godfrey. *America in Our Time: From World War II to Nixon. What Happened and Why.* New York: Vintage Books, 1976.

Kennedy, David M. *Over Here: The First World War and American Society.* New York: Oxford University Press, 1980.

May, Elaine Tyler. *Homeward Bound: American Families in the Cold War Era.* New York: Basic Books, 1988.

Nugent, Walter T.K. *Modern America.* Boston: Houghton Mifflin, 1973.

Parrish, Michael E. *Anxious Decades: America in Prosperity and Depression, 1920–1941.* New York: Norton, 1992.

Patterson, James T. *Grand Expectations: The United States, 1945–1974.* New York: Oxford University Press, 1996.

Photographic Histories

Andrews, Owen, Elliott C. Douglas, and Lawrence L. Levin. *Vietnam: Images from Combat Photographers.* Washington, DC: Starwood Publishing, Inc., 1991.

Daniels, Pete, Merry Foresta, Maren Stange, and Sally Stein. *Official Images: New Deal Photography.* Washington, DC: Smithsonian Institution Press, 1987.

Delano, Jack. *Photographic Memories.* Washington, DC: Smithsonian Institution Press, 1997.

Galassi, Peter, and Susan Kimaric, eds. *Pictures of the Times: A Century of Photography from the New York Times.* New York: Museum of Modern Art, 1996.

Greenough, Sarah, Joel Snyder, David Travis, and Colin Westerbeck. *On the Art of Fixing a Shadow: One Hundred Years of Photography.* National Gallery of Art and the Art Institute of Chicago: Washington, DC, 1989.

Guimond, James. *American Photography and the American Dream.* Chapel Hill: University of North Carolina Press, 1991.

Middleton, Harry. *LBJ: The White House Years.* New York: Abrams, 1990.

National Archives Exhibition Staff. *The American Image: Photographs from the National Archives, 1860–1960.* New York: Pantheon, 1979.

Ohrn, Karin. *Dorothea Lange and the Documentary Tradition.* Baton Rouge: Louisiana State University Press, 1980.

Roeder, George H., Jr. *The Censored War. American Visual Experience During World War II.* New Haven: Yale University Press, 1993.

Spaulding, Jonathan. *Ansel Adams and the American Landscape: A Biography.* Berkeley: University of California Press, 1995.

Stewart, Charles C., and Peter Fritzsche. *Imagining the Twentieth Century.* Urbana: University of Illinois Press, 1997.

Trachtenberg, Alan. *Reading American Photographs: Images as History, Mathew Brady to Walker Evans.* New York: Hill and Wang, 1989.